D1716459

Gardens Make Me Laugh

Gardens Make

James Rose

Me Laugh

A New Edition

The Johns Hopkins University Press
Baltimore and London

An earlier version of *Gardens Make Me Laugh* was published by Silvermine
Publishers (Norwalk, Connecticut) in 1965.

The Johns Hopkins University Press
701 West 40th Street
Baltimore, Maryland 21211
The Johns Hopkins Press Ltd., London

The paper used in this publication meets the minimum requirements of American National Standard for Information Sciences—Permanence of Paper for
Printed Library Materials, ANSI Z39.48-1984.

Library of Congress Cataloging-in-Publication Data

Rose, James.
    Gardens make me laugh / James Rose.—New ed.   p.   cm.
    ISBN 0-8018-3861-4 (alk. paper)
    1. Landscape architecture.   I. Title.
SB472.4.R67   1990
712—dc20   89-36437 CIP

Contents

Pst. Pst.
I haven't asked permission,
but I think noone will object
if I dedicate this book to you.
Of course, when I say YOU,
I really mean the sergeant in us all—
that grown-up,
"fearless,"
straight-thinking,
muscle-bound,
one-track,
loud-mouthed,
authoritarian,
twisted,
indoctrinated indoctrinator—
who, with all his childish antics,
even his own mother can't believe that he was once a baby.
When HE struts through the landscape,
sparrows fall and raindrops come to attention.

Prologue

Have you ever noticed that all garden books start with a poem? That kills me. I don't know why they do it. I guess it's supposed to show what a lofty, far-away subject they're dealing with. I'll admit that most gardens are pretty far from the everyday scene. Even in Japan they're farther away from the average person's doorstep than most Americans imagine. But I don't see what that has to do with poetry. You can't versify a garden into existence. The poem is just a substitute, a combination of words—someone else's words at that—and the book is saying, "See! I haven't done my lesson, but I brought you a wonderful substitute so that you won't notice I haven't done my lesson." It's embarrassing.

Gardens do have a language, but it isn't made up of words. In fact, words stand in the way of gardens. Of course there are other things in the way of gardens, but I think words come first because they symbolize the other things. We hide behind them. If you want to say something in gardens, you can't hide behind words. You've got to learn how to talk to a rock. And don't think I don't know how crazy that sounds—someone sitting there, talking to a rock—but I'll bet you've never tried it. That's why it sounds so crazy. But rocks make wonderful conversationalists.

Especially because you don't have to use words which get everything mixed up.

I'm a complete snob where rocks are concerned. I won't talk to just any rock. Some rocks have a lot to say if you let them. But you have to let them. You can't just go up to a rock and say, "Hi, fella. What do you think of the world situation?" That's people talk, and you'll get nowhere that way. Not with a rock. It's not because rocks are so smart. They aren't. But you've got to speak *their* language and their language is nonverbal. You don't *say* anything. You just see a rock that looks interesting. Maybe it's long, or flat and grubby, but it looks as though a lot of things have happened to it. Then maybe you say to yourself—not the rock—"I wonder what that damned rock has in mind for me?" I'm pretty sure that rocks don't have "minds." But they have something. And they do things to you if you let them, if you keep looking at them and keep words out of the conversation.

With a lot of rocks, it's better just to leave them alone where they are. But there are some rocks that won't leave *you* alone. They don't want to be where they are at all. They can't say what they want to say where they are. Or rather, they can't be what they want to be. And eventually they will tell you how and where they want to be if you listen. Of course, some rocks are just plain ornery about telling you anything. I had one once that was like a clam, but about the size of a whale. It wouldn't say anything to me. I hated that rock. If I'd seen it in a field, I'd have looked the other way. But you never see a rock like that in a field. It was strictly the kind of rock you find when you start bulldozing around the place where a garden is going to be. It sits right there in the middle of everything, half in and half out of the ground, and it won't budge—just sits there with a bare round face and not so much as an expression.

When you get a rock like that, the client always becomes very interested. Not because he likes the rock or gives a damn about it one way or the other, but because it's costing him dough—lots of it—to have bulldozers and workmen and cranes poking around it for days on end without budging it. After about the second day, this particular client started wringing his hands. It was really rough on him because there was no one to blame. I understood his position and almost felt sorry for him until he started working on me. He knew I didn't put the rock there all right, but he also knew it was costing him a fortune, and so he picked a time like that to go aesthetic. He brought out all the books—particularly the Japanese ones showing rocks and more rocks—and gave me all the arguments about gardens and rocks and I said "Yes, but not *that* rock." He thought I was just plain stubborn, but he couldn't say anything because he hated the rock as much as I did. Finally, I said, "I'll speak to it," and this nearly sent him off the cliff.

Of course I knew there was no chance of reasoning with that particular rock, but the next morning we did get it out of the ground. By noon, we had it swinging in mid-air from a crane. It looked pretty good in that position, but it was impractical. I guess it didn't want to stay there, anyway, because—I don't know how it happened—it slipped out of its chain and bounced against another rock about one-tenth its size, but in such a peculiar way that the big rock split in two, the long way. To say the least, it was peculiar. But now I had two rocks on my hands.

I'd been handling the workmen with kid gloves. That kid-glove treatment they see through like cellophane. Workmen hate this kind of situation. They hate it. And when the rock broke in two, they all looked at me as it I'd done it. I looked at the rock, because I couldn't face the workmen, and do you know that rock started saying something to me? The way it had broken was like a whale that had propagated like an amoeba. Multiplication by division, if you see what I mean. I was really impressed. The offspring weren't anything like the parent. If not handsome, they were at least curious, with fantastic shapes—unbelievable really—as natural as a baby when you get used to the idea of new babies.

It was equally fantastic the way the mother rock had disappeared. I could swear it was her way of saying something. Anyway, I listened. It wasn't exactly listening, either, but there's no word for it in English. Rock language is very difficult to translate so I'm not going to try. But it made the workmen very happy, after all they had been through, when I told them that all they had to do now was to push the new rocks into a reasonable position without carting them away. By the end of the day, even the rocks looked happy—as though they had always been there. One of them looked positively majestic, like an ancient throne in an emperor's garden. It was an inviting throne. Even the workmen gravitated to it and perched there like birds after a long flight.

The client, of course, was completely mystified. He came home looking like a hard day at the office, but when he saw the big rock wasn't there anymore, he became almost ecstatic. I think he got the emperor message, too, but he didn't mention it. He was sort of tongue-tied, I guess, because he just kept repeating, "However did you do it?" half embracing me in his awkward way. It annoys me after a while when people keep saying the same thing over and over—especially when it's "However did you do it?" and finally I said, "I spoke to the rock." For a moment after that I thought he was going to be serious, but then he broke into a wild laugh that was almost hysterical. He thought I was joking.

Gardens Make Me Laugh

A Garden Is . . .

That's the way it is with gardens and all the things that go into them, including the people. You can't explain them in words. When you think of all the garden books that have been written—and read—and all those magazine articles, and then when you think of how difficult it is to find even a decent American garden, let alone a great one, it's disheartening. I don't think it's entirely because garden books start with a poem, either. More likely it's because they ever start at all. Words are the wrong medium. Particularly garden-book words. They have a special twist that turns them farther away from gardens than ordinary words. For instance, one thing you can depend on in a really "serious" garden books is that, somewhere along the way, it will sneak in that quotation from Francis Bacon. You know the one. It's always the same. The one about people coming to build well before they learn to garden finely. The theory is that landscaping is a higher form of art than building because it always comes later than building as an art form in the pattern of a civilization's growth.

This is certainly a pretty thought from the point of view of a seventeenth-century gentleman. I don't know whether it's an eternal truth. I hope not, but I'd prefer to read my Bacon straight, to consider it in context. I might even believe it from his point of view. But when I have it warmed over for me in a garden book telling me how to keep my tuberous begonias happy over winter, I just get bored. I'm likely to look out the window at all those miserable development houses scattered over our landscape, with no gardens at all, and wonder if the people in those houses have any idea how long it will be before they have a fine garden if Bacon was right.

People don't think like Bacon any more. Gardens don't mean the same thing. Words don't mean the same thing. You can't tie them down so neatly. There are so many words floating around meaning nothing, or meaning something else, that almost the only important thing left is what you are *not* saying with them. That's why I'm not going to try to tell anyone what a garden is, or anything like that. Not in words, anyway. A garden just *is,* and all the definitions in the world won't make it one if it's not. I'd like to define a garden, all right. I think it might be fun. But to define a garden properly, I'd have to borrow a certain mirror from a Japanese friend of mine, who has a perfect mirror. That is, as nearly perfect as a mirror can get. It has only one flaw. That's when you look into it.

I think that's the best way to define a garden. Take as nearly perfect a mirror as you can get and let people look into it. Not at their faces, of course. Not even at their gardens. But at themselves, the way they are—not the way they look. And how they got that way, that's most important. But you have to do it with a mirror. You can't do it with words. Words are too slow. By the time you finish that wonderful sentence—the one that's going to hold gardens in place, like Bacon's, while you examine them—everything has changed. And if you try again and again, you just end up with a lot of definitions. If you have enough definitions, it's almost the same as having no definitions at all, but by that time you can't let it alone and more and more definitions grow up around it and finally you have to admit that it's indefinable.

With a mirror you sometimes get it, or at least part of it, in a flash. But you and I don't trust flashes. We trust words. Even the most imperfect mirror will show how we trust words. We can't help it. That's the way we are. It's got to be written. We like words, we're used to them, and somehow we got that way—so much so and for so long that by now we're very brave about words. We can risk anything with them—except indefinition—if you see what I mean. It's almost better not to have a garden than not to know how to say one. And if you know how to say one, you can file it away—on video or microfilm, perhaps—where it will be safe and you will always have it. Then you don't have to bother with a garden.

Oh, I have wordy definitions of a garden, all right. Lots of them. I even like some of them—particularly the one about a garden really being sculpture. Not ordinary sculpture, of course. Not the kind of sculpture that someone makes in a studio and then you walk around it and admire it from all the different angles, and mostly you have to think away everything else to see what the sculptor had in mind. I don't mean that kind of sculpture. A garden is much bigger. Bigger in size, at least. You can walk through it. You are inside something. You have to feel you are inside of being outside of something trying to think everything else away. A garden is sculpture from any place you are in it, even while you are in motion, and there's nothing outside that has to be thought away because that's part of it, too—just as you are.

You may not agree with my definition. You may come right out and say it's a lot of nonsense. Where are the flowers and all that? Of course, if you mention flowers at this point, I'm going to feel a little sorry for you. I'll probably talk to someone else until you become garden-broken, so to speak. Not only that. I *like* my definition. The trouble is that even

the best definition is not the thing itself—not the experience. You always have to define something in terms of something else. I happen to like this particular definition because it gets close to my idea of what a garden is. That a garden is sculpture says something to me. It says a lot. Of course, I'm very skeptical about what *you* may read into it, what *you* may mean by sculpture. So the only thing to do is to define sculpture so we will be perfectly sure. Of course, we will find that sculpture is something else—by definition. By *rights*, sculpture should be a garden now, but obviously it is not. It's sculpture—at least until we make it into a garden.

You can go on forever, substituting one word for another. Eventually, you might even prove that gardens are really words. But I think you have to be a lot more specific. I doubt there is any definition that all gardens fit into, unless it is a feeling and a way of looking at things, and even then yours is probably different from mine. When I try to make my garden-is-scupture definition fit Japanese gardens or French gardens or Italian gardens, it doesn't seem to work at all. I'm not so sure it even fits my own gardens. It's more like a wish than a definition. You have to be more specific. You have to know where the garden is and when it was built and what the people were like—not just the owners, but the workmen and the neighbors, the cop on the corner, and the people down at City Hall—and how they got that way—because that explains the way they see things and how they feel about them and the kind of gardens they are likely to get.

So if I can't tell you what a garden is, I certainly can't tell anyone how to do one. The magazines are always doing that. They've been doing it for years. And if you don't know how to do it by now, it's a hopeless situation. Anyway, I don't *know* how to do it the way the magazines do. I don't think there is any *way* to do it, if we're talking about the same thing. I should say there is *every* way to do it, but just to find one is a long process—a lifetime, as far as I know—and that's why I don't read the magazines any more, not even when my own stuff is in them.

There are some things you can tell a person how to do and some people you can tell how to do them. But these are things that have been done a million times and people who already know how to do them. The Japanese are great at that. Especially in gardens. They've been doing the same garden for so long it's become automatic. I mean like speech. In fact, a garden is a lot like speech—without words, of course—but with the same kind of play you get in conversation between people who really know how to play it. It's like fencing when people really know how to fence. It can't be a one-sided affair. Then it's no fun. It's murder. But gardens and conversation and fencing are games. They're games where two people have the same mind. Their minds come together, like an image in a mirror, and you can't fool it because it's the same mind.

But you don't play gardens with words and you don't play conversation with foils any more than you play fencing with trees or stones. They each have their own language. And if you want to see something terrible, just watch people who don't know the language trying to play any of these games. Sometimes it's terrible even if they do know the language, but can't "get with" the situation—what's happening all around —or if they just *know* the language and don't feel it, or get all mixed up in it because they've got something else on their mind. It's even better not to know the language so well as long as you don't have something else on your mind. The language is only one element. It's the tool. And it's painful to watch someone with a beautiful set of tools trying to do something he or she has no feeling for. That's really painful.

I guess that's why people always speak better in their first language the one they learned before "thinking" about it. They know things in it. They sense in it. They "mirror" in it, if they haven't got

something else on their mind. It's easy. It's automatic. And if you really want to play gardens, it has to be like that, too. You have to find the language the way you found the first language, and I don't mean from how-to-do-its. You play with trees and earth and rocks and water, but there are other things. There is a place that's already there. It's part of the game, too. You've got to *let* it be there or you spoil the fun. You're fencing a dummy instead of the person in the mirror. And the person in the mirror is you.

Rocks and trees, an unknown place and you! Now go ahead. Do something. Draw them out. You've always imagined yourself capable of any situation. Do something. Or better yet, *be* something. If you do something, you're sure to spoil it again. Words will get you nowhere in this company. I said that a garden was *like* speech, that the game was *like* conversation. Not that it *was* either. I could have said that a *great* garden was more like silence than like speech, but I'm a kindly person, and I didn't say that. But it is. It's the luxury of not saying something. It's the "something" between the lines.

The magazines never tell you how to do that. I'd like to see the magazine article that told you how to do that. I'm not going to see it, of course, because they're not going to do it. But that's where everything is—in the silence and the nothing. The "language" just barely holds them together. The magazines don't know that. They want to tell you *about* something. It's big business. Their business. It's terrifying. They have to produce something new and exciting every month of the year. A lot of work goes into it, a lot of strain. A lot depends on your martini quotient. Soon, you come up with a brilliant idea like an article I recently saw called, "How to Make Your *Nothing* Room a *Something* Room." It should have been called, "How to Make Your *Nothing* Room a Real *Nothing*." I'm serious. In more ways than one. Of course, they'd have to start with the "after" picture. (Boy, was that a nothing!) And then they'd have to leave the next page absolutely blank. There's not an editor in the world who could do it. Not in the how-to-do-it world.

I know we all have to learn how to speak. I know we have to learn how to keep quiet. We have to learn how to do gardens. These things don't just come out of the blue. I know that. Nothing does—not even nothing, particularly that between-the-lines kind of "nothing" which is really "something" by any definition. But you're supposed to pick these things up kind of early. If you don't pick them up early, the chances are that you won't pick them up. They'll be like a *second* language when they're definitely a "first." Then you have a terrible problem. And when a lot of people have a terrible problem, you have a terrible situation. You find middle-aged people all over the place, rushing around to the magazine stores, trying to find out how to do things they should have thrown away in the third grade.

The magazines don't tell you how to do a garden. They tell you how to *copy* a garden. And boy, if that doesn't stop the game, it just can't be stopped because it's the end. It's something like one of those correspondence courses in painting where you buy a canvas that's all mapped out like a jigsaw puzzle with numbers where you're supposed to put the colors in. A complete stereotype that Mr. and Mrs. Stereotype can take to the garden club, or the PTQ, or wherever they take them, and define the hell out of it. I think it's sad. I think it's sad when grown up people go around acting like that and have to read magazine articles about how to do it in the bargain.

I think it's even sadder when this kind of nonsense becomes the accepted way—meets with "approval," if you want a good magazine word for it—when if the same people ever had anything worth saying or worth keeping quiet about, they'd have to hide somewhere until it was all over. They'd hide in the garage, no doubt, with no one to tell them how to do it or how not to do it, or even where. I'm not sure, but I think this is what interests me. How we got that way. How we got in that garage—somewhere between the Cadillac marked "his" and the one marked "hers," trying to find out what to do with a stone and a tree and an unknown place.

PART I

The Mysterious West

YOU

I do hope that I haven't given the impression that now I'm going to tell you about flowers. I'm not. Not that I have anything against flowers. I haven't. They remind me more of funerals than they do of gardens, but I can't help that. It's a question of association, I guess, and I don't expect you to understand all my associations any more than I understand some of yours. But I do want to mention *something* about flowers   and then I promise not to mention them again—because it illustrates a point about something else. Not about flowers or gardens, either. About people, perhaps. I'm not sure. I'm not sure it has any point at all, but a long time ago a friend of mine—a big flower grower on the West Coast, one of the biggest—wanted me to become an East Coast representative of his company. He had other representatives. Many of them. Little people, mostly, who would take orders for him from their friends and neighbors, and then they would get a commission when their orders were filled. It seemed curious to me that, according to his own stories, so many of these little people failed. Finally I asked him how come if it was such a good business, so many of the little people failed and he said that it was because they loved flowers instead of money.

I don't know why I always remembered that. I have a terrible memory, but that impressed me. Perhaps it was because I was very young and my friend was very successful and I was trying to find a way. Perhaps it was because a lot of other things were happening at the same time. Steinbeck had just written *The Grapes of Wrath* and everybody, including my friend, was reading it. Another fellow—his name I can't remember—had just written a government report in the form of a poem called *The River.* It was quite a remarkable poem when you consider it was made up almost entirely of just facts and figures about the Mississippi River and what was happening with it—how the soil from half the United States was being carried down the river because of the way people were using the land without any regard for what happened afterward. A lot of things like that were going on, but I found it didn't make much difference in the flower-growing business. If you were going to be a big grower, you had to have lots of land—thousands of acres— and no land is good for growing for more than a few years unless you rehabilitate it, and that's expensive. So if you love money, instead of flowers, the only thing you can do is to use your land for a few years and then move on to a fresh piece that doesn't require rehabilitation.

Well, I don't love flowers *or* money, as far as I know, but for some reason I stayed out of the flower business and became a landscape architect instead. Even now—perhaps especially now—when people ask me why, I can't tell them, unless it's that if you take long enough to make up your mind what you want to do, you find yourself doing something and you don't know why. Only one thing is fairly certain—that whatever you finally do, you can never do it in a vacuum. At some point, you realize that you are right in the middle of a great big sea, mostly of people, and you haven't much to say about what it's like. It just is. And you are in it. Some people call this "the culture," and that seems to me like a pretty good name for it because it reminds me of a kind of jelly substance, found in petri dishes, where all manner of little things grow and do whatever they are going to do.

The American culture has a landscape art. In fact, it has two—one created by the artist and one that happens anyway; the one found in books, and the one you see from your window; the one of lectures and color slides, and the one commuters talk about on their way to work; the one planned for the future, and the one that happens while we sleep; the one we diagram on a piece of paper, and the one that wrote *The Grapes of Wrath*; in short, the one that's found in people's minds and far-off places, and then the one we live with.

You might think that the art would develop out of what is happening to the landscape. But it isn't like that. The art develops out of what has already happened to people. In our society, the landscape art has become a kind of fringe profession, like crime and prostitution—periph-

eral and spotty, while the other is the hard core of Americana—and yet, as with so many untried flights into the unknown, there isn't anybody—not anybody—who doesn't believe that he (or she) could be a howling success at it if he chose to abandon his mind in that direction. In a way, I agree. The trouble is that they don't know how to abandon their mind. They just sit there in this petri dish, like people watching a play—like towners—never getting into the act, and all the while imagining how great they would be if they were up there performing. I offer as witness the subject I know best—YOU—sitting there, bright-eyed and intelligent, trying to get with a garden.

My telephone rings. I'm so terrified I can't answer it. (Pavlov calls this a conditioned reflex in his experiments with dogs.) I'm terrified because I know it may be a new client. (Ask not who the client may be, for no man is a garden unto himself. The client is you.)

I know very well that on the other end of the line is someone who in some way—in every way—is, like myself, a product of western thought and culture. Perhaps a business executive, a doctor, a lawyer, a school teacher—it makes little difference. The attitudes will follow the same pattern. After about the third ring and a lightning chain of misgivings, I summon courage to answer. I, too, am something of a puritan. I know perfectly well it's a sin not to listen with an open mind—particularly when a job is in the offing—even though all my instincts tell me not to be a fool.

If it's really YOU on the other end of the line, a little game begins. We both know the rules—western rules—but this time I have the edge. You have called me, and I have more practice at this game because I play it every day. You play it every day, too, but today we are playing in my court. That gives you amateur standing.

First we identify. As guest, you serve: "Is this the landscape architect who? . . . well I'm ME . . . No, no, not *me* . . . This is a very special ME . . . After all, an ordinary *me* would go to the local plant nursery (and I may do just that if you're not interested . . . It's not so bad . . .), but so and so recommended you, . . . and we saw your work at . . . and we've decided we want you . . ." Yes, it's YOU alright. I'd know you anywhere.

In a situation like this I always try not to interrupt what may be a eulogy. Of course, I know the purpose is not to tell me how wonderful *I* am. You have a different purpose. But a very definite one. Right now, you're finessing me, and I realize this is a step you have to go through. But I'm pretty good with the backhand, and just when the ball is in that certain position—neither up nor down—I say something like, "What's your problem?" This always has a sobering effect. It's a professional secret, but I don't mind giving it away, that once you understand the problem the solution is usually built in. But my question usually leads to stammering on the other end of the line. Also a concealed annoyance with me for being so mundane as to talk about problems when beauty is really the subject. In fact, this is such a shattering question that it often acts as a catalyst in separating the different types of YOU. The responses, however, resolve themselves into surprisingly few basic types:

Descriptive. This is the most usual and, in general, satisfactory. It ranges from a glowing account of paradise, imagined or real: "We have fifty acres in Swells County with a river that forms a kind of lake in front of us with the most glorious view to the mountains . . . We love it . . . (In that case, why call me?) . . . Well, there's talk of a new highway . . ."

(Ah, the Cherry Orchard)—to an abject recital of forlorn hopes— "Ours was the only house when we moved into this development, I mean 'community,' and now they're . . . and tomorrow the driveway man . . . and our new neighbors . . . and the water tower . . . and I have to work . . . and my wife says. . . ." (Brother.)

Style-conscious and Restless. "We have a Chinese motif in the bedroom and would like to recall it in the garden . . ." (Why?). Or, "We have a 'traditional' house (whatever that is), and I was wondering if your type of work would 'fit in' . . .?" (It might fit in with the house, I'm not so sure about with YOU.) Or, "Do you do Japanese gardens?" (Of course. Whereabout in Japan do you live?) "Modern?" (I don't use words like that). Or, "We want something exciting and different . . . and we thought . . ." (Why don't you try something sensible? It will be the most exciting and different thing in your community).

Impressive. "This is G. G. Blaine of H.B.D. & O. We're building a series of new factories throughout the United States and will eventually select a landscape architect . . . I wonder if you would submit. . . ." (No, but please call me if I should be fortunate enough to be your selection.) Or, "I'm calling for Mr. Busy Big . . . You understand that you would, of course, be working directly under my supervision. . . ." (I'd like to try something like that next September. It looks like a dull season, anyway).

Sympathy Seeking. "I'm a school teacher . . . and you know what their salaries are. . . ." (Yes, I do, I teach also.)

"Practical." We just want a plan from you . . . that's all . . . (He's been reading the magazines). . . . We may not 'execute' it . . . completely, that is . . . for several years . . . (What a clever choice of words for "slow death") . . . but we want the 'art' work from you. . . ." (Boy!)

Dissatisfied. "We tried to reach you last spring, but . . . (I was hiding). . . . Well, things are in a terrible mess. . . . We've had three landscape architects . . . and none of them seems to know what he's doing. . . . (Watch out for this one. The dangerous type, looking for a fourth, and I don't mean for bridge.)

There may be other types, but most of them turn out to be a new twist to one of these categories. Hardly anyone ever says, "We know what the problems are, all right. We live here. That's part of the problem. . . ." Or, "I just can't put my finger on the trouble . . . I guess I just haven't that many fingers . . . but we'd like you to come out and give us an opinion. . . ." (This grinds my heart to tiny pebbles.) But whatever the approach, it reveals the climate of attitudes in which an American landscape is born—at least the professional one.

It Got That Way

Even from this distance I can hear you saying, "It's the same all over the world." (Yes, YOU would say that.) Well, it is, and it isn't, because the *place* is also the *society* that inhabits it. It's part of the American genius to think of these separately (and part of its dilemma to bring them together). We start with a cow path and a sacred belief in the importance of its separate parts. We're very practical. Food, shelter, and clothing come first. For it is so written. And that's the part of the cow path that we get—and that's the part we keep. Refinements come later. Then, we get good food, good shelter, and good clothing, but it's the same old cow path—air-conditioned. Any frivolous consideration, like fun with the landscape as part of the getting, is strictly forbidden. Fun is for when you can afford it. (*Now* you may decorate the air-conditioned cow path, dear.) But you never quite make it. By that time, it is what it is—a place that is already the society which inhabits it—and the talk of finery-to-come fools no one because the fun of it has never been part of the growing, only a position in the hierarchy of importance. (Not now, dear. Laughter'll be permitted on your thirtieth birthday, darlin'.)

I don't think these attitudes originated in a vacuum. They had some sort of parentage. We see things from our own petri dish, and that makes them look the same all over the world, but they aren't. That is, they are and they aren't. It's comforting to believe that everyone is in the same fix, but we shouldn't mistake provincialism for universality. *Local* is a kinder word than provincial because it doesn't imply mental boundaries—just physical ones—but I mean *provincial:* "I do it, therefore it is 'done'." This is a cousin to the Cartesian philosophy, "I think, therefore I am," which is a second cousin to, "If you don't think like me, you don't exist." That's provincial.

When you mention Descartes to the Japanese, you get about the same response as when you mention Ono-no–Imoko to a westerner. It suddenly becomes clear that it is possible for a fairly high culture—at least one whose gardens we admire—to develop with hardly any advice from our most sacred guideposts. Even if the Japanese were forced to study Cartesian, or any other western philosophy, they would do something to it. They would welcome it, of course. That's only Japanese. But it's hard for them to see it as a fixed point in the universe. That's a little *too* western.

It's we who have given the Japanese the reputation of great imitators. And having done so, this puts an end to the subject—for us. It's a solid fact. Something you can depend on. Isn't the history of Japanese contact with the West the history of Japanese imitation of western forms? Well, not exactly. It's more like absorption. We completely miss their selectivity, which is something like a child's examining a flower— "she loves me, she loves me not"—until the matter is disposed of. They can quite happily take over Christianity by simply omitting the ten commandments, and democracy by relegating the pursuit of happiness to its "proper place." (I suspect that when they take over Detroitism, it will be "slightly modified." They don't believe that to eat an egg it is necessary to become one. It's a disarming innocence—no hostility and no irreverence—simply their way of seeing things, and they are oblivious of the demons that will punish them for it.

I was a little worried for them at first. I guess I was more confused than worried—particularly when I saw a Christmas decoration at one of the large department stores in Tokyo. It displayed a monumental figure of Christ with Mt. Fuji as a background. I got the Mt. Fuji part almost immediately. That was just a local interpretation of history. But instead of the cherubic angels I was accustomed to in Christmas decorations, they had utterly seductive geishas floating in midair around the figure of Christ. I naturally recoiled, but a Japanese student explained that, Christ being such a noble gentleman, they figured He should have the best geisha available.

This kind of innocence is difficult to handle. We have no precedent. Where can you find innocence in western culture? We know what's right because we know what's wrong. Innocence has nothing to do with it. Innocence is neither right nor wrong. It's just innocence, and very difficult to accomplish from our petri dish. You'd think it would be easy to be innocent in a free society. But it doesn't work that way. You are free to be either right or wrong, but not innocent. Everybody knows what right is. It's the American way. It's very broad-minded, too. It includes imitation, plundering the land, building developments, bringing castles from Europe and gardens from Japan. It's the right way and the wrong way at the same time. And it's thoroughly acceptable. Just don't try to be innocent, or you'll get into trouble.

I had some innocent clients, a young couple. They were a scream. They wanted to build a certain way. It was so crazy that nobody could fiture out a name to describe it. They used to give parties where everybody sat around trying to figure out a name, but there wasn't any word in the English or American language that even came close. They had a beautiful piece of property, and they wanted to live on it. That's all. But it was the way they wanted to do it that was so crazy. They wanted the "house" to grow out of the landscape. I put "house" in quotes because it wasn't really a house. There wasn't any word for it. It was shelter, but not "a shelter" because it was still too much the landscape for that. It wasn't just a landscape, either, because it had very sophisticated "shelter"—radiant-heat, massive roofs, and space enough so that you could do anything you might do in a house—but it wasn't what people call a "house."

The nearest anybody came to finding a name for it was "environmental complex," and that was a howl. How could you tell the grocer to send your order to an environmental complex? He'd think you were a nut, and he'd be just as well pleased if you traded somewhere else. But the grocer wasn't the first worry. These people may have been innocent, but they were serious about it and that made it even more of a howl because they had to go to the building inspector, of course, to get a building permit. He was a man who knew what a house was. This one puzzled him, but he eventually figured out which was the house and which wasn't. He gave them long, fatherly talks about building. He could see they were "innocent," and wanted to straighten them out. But they were stubborn. Not bulldog stubborn. They just wanted their environmental complex.

When the inspector realized he had a couple of nuts on his hands, he told them where the house part of their environmental complex had to go. That's another thing a building inspector knows—where a house has to go. It's any place you want it as long as it's where he says. He gets his information from a book, and the books says that the house can be anywhere you want it as long as it isn't where it ought to be. This is arrived at by an unbelievably complex juggling of arithmetic, pitting the setback line against the rear line and the side lines against each other. If the lot is anything but a rectangular shape, or if it's on a corner with one side facing a public right-of-way, or if the property straddles two townships or has any other peculiarity, this all complicates the issue and influences the juggling. It also varies from community to community, but somehow—as if by magic—after all the abacuses are put away, it all turns out the same. It's American. It's as right as an army post, slightly camouflaged, and as wrong. But it isn't innocent.

Well, this nut team—the innocent ones—managed to survive the building inspector—I don't know how. Hardly anyone else does. I guess it was because he came first and they still had their wind. Their tussle with the banker was different. The banker doesn't use an abacus. He uses a thing called trends—a kind of financial divining rod that lets him in on all sorts of secrets about what's going to happen in twenty years. That's really frightening, because he says we're going to have more and

more of these army posts, and he's in a good position to know. It works on the principle of a chain letter, except everyone sends plans to the banker instead of letters. If they were letters, they'd be of the "now I take my pen in hand" variety. If you don't know how to do that kind of plan, you can get it from a builder or a lumber company or a magazine. It doesn't make any difference how bad the plan is as long as it has that certain something that makes it right and avoids even the appearance of innocence. This tells the banker it has resale value and fits a hypothetical person who is going to come along within the twenty years.

He's pretty sure this person will come along, too, because that's part of the chain. Your neighbor sees that you have a money plan, because the banker loaned you money on it, so he makes one as near like it as he can and sends it along to the banker. Then a group of neighbors do the same, and then a developer sees shortcuts and big business in it, and then a group of developers, and it isn't long before the American house snowballs through the American landscape.

Mr. Hypothetical buys the house, all right. In twenty, or even five, years, there isn't much else for him to buy. The banker was right all along. When Mr. Innocence arrives, he looks positively idiotic with that "environmental complex" of his amid the local corn. He confuses everyone. The neighbors are intrigued, of course, but mainly by the audacity of it. They always wanted to do something like that, the way they always wanted to put a banana peel outside the bank, but they never did it. Now, if they even admire an "environmental complex," they realize it's the same thing as saying that their own house isn't so good, and they can't do that because it isn't even paid for yet. The building inspector admits privately that he'd like to have something like that, but far away where his boss wouldn't know about it. The banker, of course, would rather have money, and he couldn't care less about "environmental complexes." If he'd seen environmental complexes in his trend sheet, it would have been environmental complexes, but that's the trouble with trend sheets and divining rods. It depends on who's looking at them. It depends on how they see it. And they always see it the way they're going to see it with or without a trend sheet.

Well, by the time these two innocent clients got through with the building inspector, the banker, the contractor, the utilities companies, the neighbors, and the grocer, they had something that looked like Knopf's solution—"slightly modified." They also picked up a good sense of what was right. They were neither stupid nor rich—just innocent—so they decided that, rather than have a half-baked "environmental complex," they'd get a house. A good, respectable, American house, designed by the inspector, the banker, the neighbors, and the grocer. Now it was right. They had a little trouble with the landscaping

21

at first. "Doesn't everyone?" They had one advantage there, however. Their landscaping was so horrible that one of the magazines took it over as a challenge to show young America "how-to-get-on." The article was called, "I Came to Crutville and Found God." It was really inspirational. The banker loved it. He put it with his "trend" sheets.

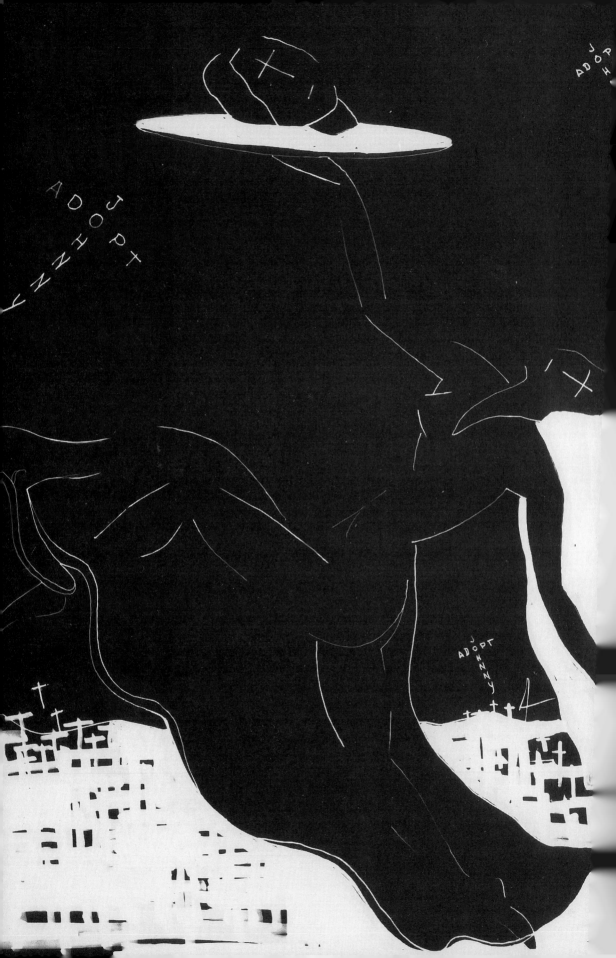

Johnny's Case

Indigenous is the word I was looking for a while ago—not *provincial,* or even *local.* (Where was it?) Well, now that I have it, indigenous seems to describe the way a thing can be local and universal without being provincial. (It also describes at least one of the qualities missing in American gardens.) And while local expression may achieve universality, as they did in Athens, the provincial has already established its boudaries and remains provincial. Conversely, that great abstraction—universality—*should* start on high with its lofty precepts and filter down to the indigenous soil. That's simple western geometry. It *should* be obeyed. But that isn't the way things work. (You see how words are? Everything is in *between* them).

Let's try an example—one that fascinates me—Billy Rose's own account of his excursion into playwriting. Being a practical man, he decided there was no mystery about writing plays, and locked himself in his room with the works of the ten most successful dramatists of our time—real money-makers. I remember that Shaw and O'Neill were among them. For weeks, he studied what made them tick. I feel certain it was an interesting study, probably quite scientific and analytical, for he came up with a series of ingredients that all these successful play-writes had in common, and they had many. On the basis of these common factors, he constructed a play of his own, and as you might guess, instead of a still life it turned out to be a "dead fish" that even bringing the American flag out in the last act couldn't save. (He must have had parts left over—the fun, perhaps.)

The great architectural experiment in this direction resulted in the International Style, which was something like trying to make a "pure" baby by assembling it out of its parts. Fortunately or unfortunately, most progeny, which spring from the contact between ourselves and our environment, are by no means so pure. They have parents and grandparents and a host of embarrassing relatives, but mostly that elusive ingredient called life, which has never quite been captured. It just is. And as long as it is, anything can happen. Every once in a while something wonderful happens—sometimes it seems just often enough to keep things going and sometimes it seems just to be—it depends on whether you want to make it fit into geometry and words or whether you are content to let it be what it's going to be. Sometimes it's horrible—mostly, perhaps.

For my own part, there's one area where I have achieved perfect contentment, and that's the area of history. History is a terrible laugh, because history is *now*. I'm perfectly content to let historians trace the influences and separate the ingredients in the potpourri of American culture, but when they get all finished, it's still a pot of stew. I *like* stew, of course. Sometimes it nauseates me, but never as much as historians poking around trying to find the overalls in it. They're repulsive. They're always trying to find out why Johnny's disturbed. How could he be anything else? Wouldn't you be disturbed if you were locked up in a pattern of geometry and words and told (for the *most* logical reasons) that you must never, never go outside where you already know that everything is? You just don't realize how lucky you are to *be* outside, free of all this nonsense, identifying so beautifully with what *is* that you don't need any logic or words to support you.

Johnny Landscape is less fortunate. He reads like the "Adopt A Puerto Rican" posters. He's not quite sure who his parents were. First, there were the British, and I'm not even going to mention them. I can't trust myself. No Irishman could. Anyway, there were others. Oodles of them. You know who they were as well as I do. The British simply get a bigger play in the history books. But if you've traveled in Germany recently, for instance, and seen all that crazy building and all the hustle, and all the progress, and all that special "properism" that the Germans have so much of (wait for the light, boy, whether there's a car coming or not or you'll have a civilian arrest on your hands) you might have the sensation that you're right back in Boston. Or when you do come back to New York from, say, Stuttgart or Cologne, don't take the subway down to Wall Street and get yourself into a myopic trance with the noise and the dirt of it and then come up suddenly into the light and find dear old Wall Street right in front of you. You'll swear that you've never left Stuttgart or Cologne, or wherever it was you first realized there may be others besides the British in the parentage that Johnny Landscape is so confused about.

These are anonymous things that happen to Johnny while he's sleeping. It's a nightmare. The poor kid should spend some time in the country with fresh air and all that. You know, where he could breathe and see more of his parentage. I don't mean just old standbys like the dustbowl. He can see that in his own backyard, now that he's moved to the suburbs. I mean something elegant. Something like that Bavarian village that William Randolph Hearst brought back to California—but not quite alive because he forgot to bring the Bavarians and that's something like Salome forgetting to bring the body when she presented John the Baptist to the king. It's hard to separate these things and still have a lively situation.

Of course, as influential as Mr. Hearst was, his idea never really took hold—not the Bavarian part of it—and I'm not really sure whether he was a leader or a follower. Everyone was doing the same thing—bringing some kind of sacrificial part of the potpourri from some other petri dish—like a castle from Scotland deposited on the shores of Miami. It was very popular. The first question your architect would ask you was what style you wanted. Some people couldn't make up their minds. They didn't know who or what they were, and sometimes ended up with each room a different style, and boy, if you want to see something crazy, you should see some of these people running from one room to another trying to be a Spanish Duke in one, and Empress Eugenia in another. No wonder they ended up in a rumpus room. You could just imagine you were right in the Place de la Concorde, and when you can do that, you've got what they call a symptom.

It got to be a way of life—and still is, except that we're way beyond castles—and a very profitable way. So profitable that the schools got in on it. After all, if you're going to do something insane, you might as well do it properly, and you need schools to show you how. Harvard lead the way, of course. They sent students all over Europe to copy every garden that's ever been done. They brought back measured drawings. They were absolutely accurate—to the millionth of an inch—more accurate, I'm sure, than the drawings of the guys who did the original gardens. Maybe they didn't even have drawings, but if they ever wanted some for any reason later on, all they had to do was to go to Harvard to find out what they'd done.

I don't mean to say that Harvard just filed these drawings away in some musty archive. Of course they did that. But there was a practical side. They trained the students, who were unfortunate enough not to get to Europe, to measure the drawings of the students who did so that, no matter what Mr. Hearst or anyone else wanted, they could "adapt" the copies of the copies of the gardens that the guy who did them originally may not even have had a drawing of. You can see how unruly this could get. The accuracy could easily be deflected with so many people copying copies and "adapting" the copied copies. This really did require straightening out, or at least systematization. But no real worry. Harvard was there. One professor wrote the bible of landscape architecture. It was the first real how-to-do-it in the field. It was a big book, of course, and very scholarly. It sort of brought things together. After that, there was no reason for anyone to go off half-cocked, like a crazy artist. You just had to read the book. Everything were there, and not between the lines, either. It was right there. The history, the drawings. Everything. You didn't even have to go to Europe, anymore. The professor had been.

You can see the advantages. For one thing, anyone who could read could learn. It got rid of vagaries such as talent. You didn't have to look at nature or people. You just had to look at the book. Salome had a busy night when that was written. It dissected everything. Well, not everything. It never mentioned the American Indian or the Aztecs or the Mayans—that's another book—it concentrated on respectable things. The Italian renaissance, for instance. The Villa D'Este. Boy, did it concentrate on the Villa D'Este. That was *it*. If you could just find a place to fit the Villa D'Este and a client like Signor D'Este, you were made. But if you couldn't find a place like that or a client like that, there was still that wonderful concept called "adaptation." Now there's a word for you: "adapt." Just think about it. One landscape architect thought about it a lot. He must have had a pen handy while he was thinking because he wrote one of the most unique lines in American literature (landscape architectural division.) He sent it to the *Landscape Architecture Quarterly*—you may not have heard of that one, but that's where he sent it—and they published it in April 1938. He said. "It is perhaps this very eclecticism—the borrowing of styles that are native to other countries and other times—that garden design in America is most obligated for its wealth of expression as an art; for in this country there is hardly a climate or geographical environment or an inherited American tradition to which some landscape architectual form, based on European precedent, cannot be appropriately adapted as a means of both utility and greater ornament." I think that's a great line, American to the core. I don't know how the core got that way, but it did.

Perhaps the professor was right. Perhaps there is something about gardens that you can *can* capture if you have the right net. At least I think we ought to be broadminded enough about it to see that if we had his identical background and upbringing and education, we would see the landscape exactly the same way. Then it would be *right*. But to understand Johnny Landscape's confusion, you have to see it from *his* point of view. He's not a professor and he doesn't know the finer distinctions between right and wrong and he's probably never even seen the book or the drawings and doesn't even know what a garden is. He only knows what happens to him, and when you get him out in the country, he's liable to see that there are other kinds of landscapes that aren't in the book at all.

First of all, there's the natural one. The professor never thought of that. Oh, he thought about it all right, but as a kind of messy business, like sex and violence, that has to be brought under control, has to be put in some kind of a logical cage. That's the way he is. The question is whether when he gets his cage, is there anything of nature left in it or does it turn out to be the Villa D'Este again transplanted to Long Island or Newport or any of the other watering spots suitable for a masquerade and to hell with the rest of it. Well, not exactly to hell with the rest of it, either. The cage is flexible, and you can always adapt to "existing conditions." This is very convenient because you can now forget about the Villa D'Este (it's hard, but you can do it) and go on to newer cages such as the split-level (an unconscious, but telling, metaphor), the ranch house, the cathedral ceiling, the atrium, and God knows what others and if He doesn't, your builder or the magazines can help Him out.

And all the while Johnny Landscape is terribly, terribly confused as to what and who he is. He doesn't know whether the cage is capturing him or nature—that is, the respectable part of nature—and which side of the cage he's on and which side nature's on. All he knows is that's the way things are and he's a goddamned disturbed kid. Every once in a while he sees something—even little things—that are confusing. An old farmhouse, for instance—one of those that started out modestly and then, when the farmer got prosperous, changed dramatically as he started doing things to it. He started thinking about it—he even read a book—and before you or he or anyone else knew about it, it became just like that painting by Grant Wood, *American Gothic,* with the farmer and his wife standing there, pitchfork in hand, perplexed about the whole thing.

Strangely, the farmer didn't think about his barn. Not in the same way. That was for cows and other animals he had to treat with respect if he wanted to get prosperous enough so that he could play masquerade with his house. Why not? Well, the cows seem to have got the better of the deal—that is, in the barn—but then they began to take over the outside, and that was okay, too, for a while—until the farmer got so prosperous that he decided to get rid of the cows and start selling the land to anyone who came along. The trouble was that everyone forgot that the cows weren't there anymore, and they started building their houses and factories and all the rest of it along the paths that the cows had designed.

In some ways, cows are better designers than people. At least they're not confused about who they are and what they are and where nature is and whether they're part of it or not. They know they're not people, but people don't seem to know they're *not* cows. People *think* they're not cows. They think about it so much that they don't know what they are. They build a kind of thinking wall to prove that they're not cows. And of course they're *not* cows. They're people. They're so much people that it seems curious they have to prove they're not cows. And I don't mean just cows. They have to prove they're not like anything that ever existed. And of course they're not (what or who do you know who would build something called "American Gothic"), but when they have to prove it by building that wall, they're really saying that they don't know what they are. They want to view it all and dissect it and analyze it and separate it and buy it and sell it and build Gothic American or split-levels or cathedral ceilings to show who they are, and pretty soon they don't know whether the wall is keeping them in or keeping them out. All they know is that they're as separate as John the Baptist's head from his body, and even Salome isn't having much of a ball.

After a while, everyone agrees that that's the way things are. Of course, you and I and the professor and the historian and the banker and the guy down the street all have different versions of it. But nobody puts John the Baptist together again. We think about it. We decorate the cow path. We build a garden (boy, that's dreaming). We console ourselves. We say it's the same all over the world. We buy a Cadillac and build a highway, lots of them, and still we can't "get with it." It's something like Alice Adams trying to fix up that goddamn awful brown room with a bunch of roses. She didn't make the room. It got that way. She's like Johnny Landscape. Disturbed. She doesn't really believe it has to be like that. But there's the wall, you know. She doesn't know whether it's meant to keep her out or keep her in. She's just separate.

Gardens Are Born

Birth is seldom easy but I understand it can be a kind of exquisite agony. The extent of the agony is impossible to foretell. I find, however, there is often a relationship between the final excellence of a work and the ease with which it is performed. But it's impossible to tell ahead of time. One of the most unlikely jobs that's come my way—a factory in New Jersey—turned out to be one of the best. I made a rough model of what I intended—a water garden in a central atrium surrounded by offices—and after a brief checking of costs, the president of the factory said, "Go ahead." It was as simple as that. There were never any "working drawings" or anything beyond this sketch model. I went at it exactly like a sculptor. During construction, I noticed that brass pipe and copper sheeting were available from stockpiles of material used in the factory, and suggested that a fountain could be made from these. Working with craftsmen employed in the factory, we designed and built a fountain especially for that interior courtyard. We also experimented with copper lanterns and lighting fixtures. I had no idea what any of this was going to *look* like, but I had a very good feeling about what I hoped it would *be* like. So I allowed it to happen, and pretty soon it was like I always knew it would be—as it "wanted" to be.

33

On another occasion, I had an equally good, or better, client situation—except. The clients were devoted—to the point of embarrassment. They waited for me for nearly a year while I was visiting in Japan. I didn't realize they were waiting, and on my return, I neglected to call them immediately, but they were very cheerful about it. Since it was already late in the planting season, I selected a dozen or so trees—among them an apple tree that was nice enough for children to play in, and that fit the space perfectly as a major element in the design—to be dug and held at the nursery until we could get to planting. The clients gave me carte blanche and the question of money was never discussed. To top all this, they announced that they would go on vacation during construction of the garden.

You might think this an ideal situation, and it was, in a way—except. Except they were slightly apprehensive about minutiae—about the way the screening would fit the porch, the pattern of the brick, and above all, if it would seem contrived (not if I could keep them out of the design department). Of course, I played these apprehensions down. After each meeting with them, their list of anxieties (sometimes written) dissolved miraculously, as anxieties should. But I find that some people *like* their anxieties, and won't be cheated out of them so abruptly. These particular anxiety-carriers wanted to see another garden I had done—and this is always a mistake—but I fell right into the trap.

The meeting of the two sets of clients was apparently a cozy affair in which garden making was dissected in some detail—an anxiety-fest where apprehensions, past and present, were given free rein. It seems that the clients with the garden already built had an apple tree—an existing one, not one that I had planted (but anything will serve if you're looking for anxieties)—and that particular apple tree was too friendly with some yellow jackets that inhabited it. After that, I could never convince the new clients that yellow jackets and apple trees weren't a package deal. They did, however, give up the yellow jacket argument eventually because they had acquired a lot more ammunition than that. They had also discovered that apple trees have apples and that apples fall to the ground and apples on the ground can be a messy thing (depending on how you look at it), and if you want something to be anxious about, that's as good as anything else. I could have given them more ammunition—tent caterpillars for the cherry trees, bronze borers for the birches (to say nothing of leaf miter)—but what's the use?

This, of course, is a glorious chain—I call it the anxiety chain—and like the good chain it is, it never ends. For instance, in my own innocence, I took quite a liking to eucalyptus trees in California until a client nearly left this world because I used them. They were "dirty" trees, he said, because they shed their bark. I was also once naive enough to admire ailanthus trees—the trees that grow in Brooklyn—which are considered an ancient and honorable tree in China where they came from. I even thought I had a great find because they grow so fast and have such an exotic shape and you can practically grow them in concrete and they can be literally pulled out of any field and replanted at practically no cost. I couldn't see why anyone who wanted a beautiful tree shouldn't have one. But, when I tried to use one for a client who called himself a "charity case," he would have none of it because the female of that species has a slight odor for a short period during the summer, and in the part of Brooklyn he came from, the kids used to call them "stink" trees.

For a time I groped my way along the anxiety chain—trying to "please"—until a couple of enlightening things happened. First—to reinstate the dignity of ailanthus—an indecently rich, but nonetheless parsimonious, client of mine *insisted* upon having ailanthus trees on his yacht-landing-terrace because he clearly saw how he could save a buck and because, at the same time, no one in his circle would dare call his propriety to account. But the one that really got me off the chain for keeps was the client that sent me down to North Carolina to get the feel of his summer place so I could better make it "fit in" to the rest of the countryside. While there, I noticed how beautifully the catalpa trees grew in that locale and recommended several on his landscape plan. He vetoed them—not unhysterically—saying they were "darkie" trees.

But the chain goes on. And on. Because of it, not one-tenth of the trees—beautiful trees—that could be used are even grown any more. There's the yellowwood tree, *Cladrastis lutea,* which has flowers like wisteria, bark like an athlete's skin, and foliage like the night. But you can't find it. No one grows it because somebody said it was "brittle," whatever that means. The common mulberry tree is another a gorgeous thing that must have been fashioned out of oriental fables, but you can't use it—bird droppings, you know. Or take the scholar tree. No one else wants it (I haven't figured out why, unless it's that egghead name and they're afraid of osmosis, but it's practically extinct for landscape purposes). And on and on it goes, until you have left about three trees that are considered properly respectable. I think the maple is one, but not all forms of that, either—just that old sugar maple, and perhaps the Norway, which always reminds me of apples on a stick.

I wish this peculiar landscape viewing were as simple as a few hysterical prejudices about trees, but I'm afraid it isn't. These are only symptoms of an impossible dilemma. Everyone wants to have and have not at the same time. They want flowers without bees, leaves that never fall from the tree, gardens without the nuisance of nature's butting in.

They want to separate the ingredients and still have the cake, which is a very difficult trick to accomplish. Aesthetics are one thing, and practicality another. They're both quite different from materials. And all these are quite separate from the time and place. They're particularly separate from the great "I am," who makes all these distinctions and classifications and who imagines he is getting "at" something, and he is. But not *with* it.

In a society where people see themselves as part of the natural process, those with such odd notions about their environment would be mercifully institutionalized. But we all know that people have a perfect right to be insane as long as they do it in the accepted manner. It does lead to some problems when such a person decides that now he wants a garden. He can't see why he shouldn't have one if he can afford it. After all, isn't a garden another possession, like a Cadillac—a status symbol, perhaps? So let's *have* some "art." Let's be broadminded about it. Well, this leads to some interesting situations. No one is going to deny anyone a garden—particularly one whose business is garden-making—but the only way that such a person can get a garden, even if he or she is ready, willing, and able, is to be tricked into it. This leads to a kind of play within a play. The dramatis personae looks something like this:

Characters (in order of appearance)

The Client   (usually a husband and wife team with a various assortment of children, continually on and off stage. This is YOU).

The Site   (at the beginning of the play, this is usually a terrible mess. Something has happened to bring it all to a head. Anyway, it's there, and no one knows what to do about it).

The Cheat   (that's me. Nobody understands what I do, not even me).

Others   (the workmen, an occasional "expert," neighbors, various officials, sidewalk kibitzers, magazine editors, photographers, and the public).

In the opening scene, we all sit around, very broad-minded, discussing your "problem"—YOU always have a problem. You're very logical, of course, so it takes some time to get at what the problem is. In discussing the problem so openly and broad-mindedly, it is often revealed that the husband and wife have entirely different problems. They didn't realize this before because in the fifteen years they've been married they've worked out ways to avoid this very discussion. It's always the same problem, though. It's YOU, trying to get with it or get away from it or somehow to react to the site.

The "site," of course, is a word-substitute we use instead of experiencing the natural environment. The site, itself, has very little to do with nature, anymore. It's simply what we see when we look out of the window, and that's liable to be different for everybody, because all of us see it through our own conditioning and so naturally it's a different problem for everyone. It has one thing in common with almost everyone today and that is that it's "out there," and that's why it's a problem.

I've heard this broad-minded discussion about the problem so often that I'm not even listening. That is, I'm listening and I'm not listening. I know that if I listen, I'll probably become as righteous and logical as you are about it, and this will only preserve the problem. I also know that if I'm not listening, I may hear something that isn't the problem at all but the answer to it. This listening and not listening, I call the myopic state, and I have absolutely no idea what that is, but I find it very useful and, as far as I know, absolutely necessary, but I don't know why. I think it serves as a kind of nonsense-screen which gets rid of all the beautiful reasoning you have strangled the "problem" with in thinking about it, but I'm not sure. I only know that YOU are sitting there making broad-minded noises that usually have nothing to do with what is wrong and never have much to do with setting it right. And all this while, I know I'm listening because if you happen to falter in your line of thought, I can always prompt you—fill in the next three or four sentences—because I've heard them so often and they're always the same. I also know I'm not listening because I'm probably thinking about something far away—like the way that Greece became a garden without the help of landscape architects or clients either, for that matter.

A little later in this discussion—when the logic is growing thin and I know I will soon be expected to say something brilliant—I come up with, "Well, let's take a look at it." This is a signal for everyone to scramble outdoors. Here, we go through a similar ritual—this time it's more visual than vocal, and my position shifts from hearing and not hearing to seeing and not seeing. YOU, of course, are giving me the low-down— what has been done and by whom and what's wrong with it and how much it cost. What you like and don't like and what you saw in a magazine and who has what in the neighborhood and what you wouldn't have and where you've been and what you've seen. You're getting at the real YOU, and it's quite a portrait. I'm listening, of course, but I'm also noting the drainage situation and how the land slopes and how the property lines haven't the faintest relation to any natural boundary and how the house sticks out of the ground as if it were trying to get away and that crazy driveway trying to look like the entrance to an estate and that front door which is never used—unusable, in fact, because you can't get to it (why they bother to have front doors is a mystery—probably a refined hangover from better days)—I'm trying to figure out why you can't get from any living part of the house to the outdoors and who ever thought of that barbecue in the yard (boy!) and what the rest of the community is like and what a stinker the builder must have been and how do privileged people in the "richest country in the world" get themselves into such a mess, anyway. I'm listening, of course, while you're telling me (or are you telling yourself?) how really swell it is to live in Fairville.

Fortunately (or unfortunately), during this myopic tour of seeing and hearing, and not seeing and not hearing, I usually find a key that will unlock some pain from the situation. I don't know how or why. It happens. Something the client said while I wasn't listening or something I saw while I wasn't looking, or perhaps a combination of the two, sets up a kind of pinball reaction, which brings everything into a new relationship. It's never a specific answer—always a relationship—and this is where the client thinking is so different. The client feels only the irritation at the point of irritation (that damned fence, the neighbor's kids, or the water collecting at the base of the building). The problem is not here at all, and the answer is an entirely different kind of adjustment.

This isn't easy to convey to clients. They *know* the problem is in the specifics—the fence, the kids, the water—and they usually have to paint the fence, strangle the kids, and drain the water to find out that things are pretty much the same in Fairville. Words are useless. I can't tell them what's wrong. It's so remote and obvious and simple at the same time that it's unacceptable to them. They have to be tricked into seeing it. So I say I have to "think" about it—which is a downright lie. I *never* think about a garden. I say this to the clients. They want to be taken seriously. Their own thinking is so insane that they torture themselves and expect me to torture myself on their behalf. Well, I don't take them seriously *or* torture myself, but if I told them that the answer was right there, staring them in the face, they wouldn't believe me. They wouldn't see it. They want the full treatment, and they have to go at their own pace, but the answer is there all the while.

What may or may not happen is strictly nonverbal. As long as they think of their garden as a possession—something to be bought or sold like a Cadillac, something outside themselves, an object that results from making a composition or getting the colors and textures right or any of the other crazy things they talk about in the magazines—it can never happen. They may get an antiseptic substitute, but until they identify they have no garden. This is the only way I can help them. And considering the cast of characters in this little play—the neighbors, the "experts," the officials, the workmen, the sidewalk kibitzers, the editors, the general public, and YOU—which really represent the main currents of thought in our petri dish—each so honorable and so thoroughly a hundred percent—why, someone has *got* to cheat. That's ME. That's my job. I'm the cheat.

You're the honest one. You only cheat yourself. That's an amateur. It's really not nice, either. It's simply accepted behavior. But if you want to have a garden in your petri dish, somebody's got to cheat who knows *how* to cheat—a professional. I hope you don't think I'm talking about money, either. I'm not. I'm talking about them—all those people who have been designing your garden for you since you were a kid—and that includes everyone from the first schoolteacher who made you sing "America, the Beautiful," right down to the guy who invented that mushroom garden light. And all the characters in between, which include the neighbors and the magazines and the experts and the mason and the banker and the building inspector—everyone who knows how things "should" be done. When you get a potpourri of highly principled experts like this in your petri dish, designing your garden for you, you simply need someone who knows how to cheat. That's what you pay me for. We never mention it because we're so polite, but that's what it is. You pay me to cheat without letting you know that I'm doing it. I don't mind. I like it. I'm good at it, too. I'd even be glad to show you how I do it, except that I'm not quite sure how. I don't think about it. It just comes naturally when the situation arises. It's something like having a conversation with a rock, but more complicated. It's a game like Ouija, only you don't use a board. You don't use anything. That's what's so wonderful about it. Nothing—I mean NOTHING—happens, and there's the answer. That's because I cheat.

The very best cheating happens in that first pinball session when all sorts of signals are flashing around and decisions being made without the client's having the faintest idea of what's going on—at least no idea of the importance of what's going on. I don't mean to say that the client isn't smart. He's terribly smart. He knows what's going on all right, but he also knows how to play the game although he's not quite sure what the game is. But he has an instinct about it. He knows that if he were playing the game by himself, it would be about as dull as playing tennis against a backboard. It's just more fun with a partner. You never know what's going to happen and when the ball is coming toward you, there's no time to think about it, but that's when things are happening. The client can tell himself that this isn't very important because it's just a game. So what, if he's not very good at it? He knows that eventually you have to get down to practicalities, to finishes and surfaces—paving patterns, and all the pictures he has in mind—these are the back-boards he's been playing against and that's why the game hasn't been much fun, but the other side of him knows that something else is happening now. It's a strange experience. He feels out of control. At the same time, something tells him that all this pinball hocus-pocus—this mysterious talk about "the site" and what is there and how he comes into the picture and what he wants (or thinks he wants) and the house and the community and the drainage and the neighbors—is somehow going to determine whether or not he ends up with a garden. It hurts a little, but it's not so bad. There are acres of time to worry about the surface. It's not *really* cheating if everyone knows what's going on.

Sometimes the cheating is on a much smaller scale—petty, in fact—and *very* real. Most clients are thoroughly indoctrinated as to the sanctity of a plan. The magazines have been harping on that for years, and, in a way, it's one of their minor vices. A plan should not be tampered with, of course, but in the final reckoning, it depends on who does the tampering. Generally speaking, the client should not, and in that sense, the indoctrination has been useful. But the vicious part of indoctrination is that there's no way of stopping it. It eventually becomes a law of nature instead of a contrivance of editors. It gets to the point at which the client mistakes a plan for a garden, instead of a piece of paper, which it is, and will happily file it in a drawer marked "P," or under "A" (for art work), and then proceed to do what he was going to do from the beginning—but with a clear conscience that the magazine editor won't get him.

This allegiance also works the opposite way, which amounts to the same thing because it's still mistaking the plan for the garden. The client becomes so sold on the plan that he or she won't permit even the deviations of nature or a slight rewording by the author, so to speak. I've had it happen. One client wouldn't permit me the slightest change—not an iota (that's a poisonous weed found among cerebellums)—after the plan was set. On this particular plan, the driveway had been located by me from data on a topographical survey map (another plan that can't be trusted) and the entrance was cut through an existing hedgerow by a bulldozer operator during my absence. It was exactly according to plan. Precisely. But I saw immediately that, if the entrance had been located six or eight feet uphill, possibly serious drainage problems would be avoided in the future and the curve of the driveway would be improved. I spoke to the client about it. He was a little disturbed because that's the way it showed on the plan, but he said he'd think about it (copying my trick). Well, that afternoon while he was thinking about it, I had the bulldozer operator scoop up one bucket of the hedgerow, trees and all, from one side of the entrance, and lay it down on the other.

The next day, having thought about it, the client said to me, "I don't think I want to change the plan to move that entrance." And I said, "I guess you're right. It looks pretty good the way it is."

I consider that petty and deceitful and dishonest, and I love it. But cheating is even more fun when the client has a fixed idea. They're great. Now, a fixed idea is something that a client sees, a vision un-possessed. It's entirely outside of context with "the site," the way he lives, and the use he has for it, but he wants it—desperately—the way a kid wants a drum. It's a wonderful, far-off object which, at the moment, seems to him the elixir of happiness. In one instance, the fixed idea was San Remo. Yes, San Remo, Italy, which the clients wanted to transfer to South Orange, N.J. Not literally, of course, but the spirit and the feeling of it. One difficulty was that they had a rather small lot, and most of it was taken up by a rather large house that would never be anything but South Orange. Even if they had had acres, I couldn't have made South Orange into San Remo—there are certain differences, and I know my limitations—but even in San Remo, I wouldn't try to imitate San Remo any more than I would try to imitate South Orange in South Orange.

I suppose I could have captured some Italian surfaces and masquer-aded some bric-a-brac—a dolphin, perhaps—the way people try to masquerade their gardens as Japanese. I could have gotten a book—there probably is one—that gives you a recipe. It would be like one of those restaurants that pretends to be in the heart of Paris because they've painted a street scene on the wall and brought in an authentic lamp post. There was evidence in the decor of the house that the clients would have gone along with the idea, but I didn't do that. I cheated. I get so tired of looking for the little man who isn't there. The game doesn't interest me. It's hard enough to find the man who *is* there. It's even harder to let him *know* he's there—right there—in that garden. He *is* the garden.

During all the slide showing and the movie showing of San Remo and all the talk—there was a mountain of talk—and while I was listening and not listening and looking and not looking, something very strange happened. At least it seemed strange to me because it was completely out of character with the couple—the clients who seemed to be de-manding that I do a kind of caricature—a grimace—of San Remo in their backyard. At one point in the movie—I don't think it was even showing San Remo at that moment—the wife turned to her husband and said, "Look at that. . . . remember how we stood on that balcony and cried because it was so beautiful?" I was glad that the room was dark because I could sense the husband's embarrassment at being so exposed, but *I* wasn't embarrassed. I was enlightened. They had found

41

a place they were really *with*, and were now mistaking the experience for a canned picture of it.

After that, I forgot all the nonsense about San Remo. The talk continued, of course. And I listened—really, I listened—and finally I went out in their backyard and staked out a garden. That experience was like trying to build a nest for some birds who had forgotten how, but it came back to them as time went on. The greatest difficulty was in getting them to see that a nest has to fit the tree. Their greatest surprise was when they saw how it did fit. And now it's what I would call a real American garden, made for Americans who are living in South Orange, N.J. That's all it is. And that's quite enough. Of course, the words the clients

use to describe it are different from mine. I know because I dropped in unexpectedly late one afternoon after it was finished and they were sitting alone by the side of the pool. They said, "We love it. It's just like San Remo." Well, maybe it was, and maybe it wasn't. Some things are hard to define.

The fixed idea, of course, has more faces than one. I sometimes think it has as many as there are clients, but that's only partly true. One recurring face of the fixed idea shows itself in the form of a barbeque—that's a vision for you, everyone cooking underneath the bough—but in some communities, it assumes the proportions of an epidemic. It's a point of pride with me that I've never done a barbeque, although I've often been curious about what would happen if I found myself with no alternative. I think it might be interesting. Obviously, the cook-out situation doesn't have to be as bad as it sounds and usually is. The nearest I ever came to it turned out to be quite a different affair before the job was finished. I'm not sure how it happened, but fixed ideas are elusive.

I was called in to "do a barbeque," all right, but the voice over the telephone sounded a little tentative. I don't know how to explain it, but I do know that you *never* know from that first telephone conversation—no matter what is said—whether a job is going to be a good job or not, so I went. It seems there had been a rash of barbeques in this particular neighborhood and this new client didn't have one and so he felt left out of things and that wasn't his style at all. The neighbor immediately next door had just come up with a little three-thousand dollar monster with spits and fans and rotaries encased in stone, and that's the sort of competition you can't put up with if you live in a community exposed to a barbeque epidemic.

At our first meeting, the client almost talked barbeques out of existence—at least into something so elaborate it was hardly a barbeque any more. I was listening, of course, and by the end of the evening, that neighbor—the one with a little three-thousand-dollar barbeque—looked like the original cheapskate because we had somehow arrived at a budget of seven thousand to do one properly. Toward midnight, we were out in the backyard with a flashlight poking around among the bushes to find a suitable place for such a barbeque. I happened to mention that it would be a good idea if he had a few lights around when he got the new barbeque, and he said, "Lights?" I said, "Yes, they could be arranged in the planting . . ." and he said, "Planting?" And I think that's how it all started.

We arranged to meet at a nursery to see what there was to this planting business. Not an ordinary nursery, of course. It was more like an arboretum—one that had been established a hundred years ago—and which abounded in unusual and exotic plants, unusual because there is hardly anyone interested in growing them any more, but I could never have anticipated the client reaction. He had found his wonderland, like a child first discovering the magic of water, except he wasn't a child and it wasn't water and he wanted to possess every plant he saw. Before I could get him away from the nursery, he had bought enough for a dozen surburban lots like his and assured me I would find a place for them at his house. I must say that he loved beautiful things.

However, to love beauty is one thing, and to possess it is another (and if you don't already understand the difference, I can't explain it) but plants have a way of bringing this out in people—which side they're on. I've seen it in action—in particular, one time when I was down in Florida doing a place for a prominent house-and-home magazine. We needed some plants to spike a photograph and drove out to one of those exotic plant nurseries they have down there, but the owner wouldn't let us have any. I thought he was a nut. A real fruitcake. We were just trying to borrow some plants to put in a photograph. You've got to have plants to put in a magazine photograph. Not just ordinary plants, but the kind that make readers say "Ah" and "Oh" and "Wherever did you get *that*," and he had just that kind of plant—thousands of them—but he wouldn't let us have any. He watched us like a bird. There was the editor, with three assistants and me as consultant and a bunch of workmen—all standing around. I couldn't figure the cost per minute to have us all standing around, but the magazine's meter was clicking away and this guy was just standing there watching us like a bird. We would have paid him anything he asked and he knew it, but he just watched us and every time we got near to a plant or even walked in that direction he's say, "Not that one. Any one but that." He was a real nut. The worst part of it was that I sort of knew what he meant. I have a secret plant myself. It's a special tree, and I won't even tell anyone where it is. It's at a nursery. I'll tell you that much. I can't afford to buy it, but I have a deal with the nursery not to let anyone else have it without first giving me a chance to find a place for it. Right now, I have no place for the damned tree, but there is a place for a tree like that and a tree like that should have a place. I can't see a person having that tree just because he can afford it. That has nothing to do with it. And I think that's sort of what the guy in Florida had in mind when he wouldn't let the magazine editors possess his plants for even a few hours no matter how much they paid him. They had love on the wrong side of beauty.

When you buy enough exotic plants for a dozen surburban gardens—however interesting each of the plants may be individually—however interesting each of the plants may be individually—it's like inviting all the celebrities in the book to one party. It's got to be maneuvered constantly. My job was to maintain the semblance of a garden while keeping it from bursting at the seams. The client mercifully acquired an adjacent lot (not the one with the barbeque), but this, too, began to fill ominously. Fortunately, after the first few rapturous visits to the nursery I'd begun to hate, the buying subsided as abruptly as it started. I was bewildered, and found myself braced in the wrong direction. The clients had gone on a vacation to Miami Beach and I didn't hear from them until six months after their return. Then, the wife (lovely as a poplar) coyly showed me a newly acquired nine-carat diamond. "We fell in love with it," she said.

Of course, we'd talked about a swimming pool, as we'd talked about a barbeque (only by now I'd begun to really listen), and I could see that was next. I rather liked the idea because it represented a kind of oasis where for at least a thousand square feet, no trees or plants of any kind, exotic or otherwise—except for one enormous weeping white birch placed to reach out over the pool—could be planted. That tree with the poplar-lovely wife beside it and the water shimmering by in the sun-

light were something to behold. At moments, they all became one, and that's the test. Maybe they got on the right side of beauty after all.

But it wasn't easy. I'll even skip the first few years of it, and it wasn't easy. I guess when you're after perfection, nothing is easy. To take one small example—not the planting, which was abundant; or the terracing, which was extensive; or the play-yard, which was complete; or the lighting, which was a project; or the insect repellent, which was automatic; or the hi-fi, which was everywhere, or the pool, which was eternal—just take the paving around the pool. That ought to be simple enough. But it isn't. Not if you want perfection. It has to be skid-proof so that you don't slip on it when it's wet and your feet are bare. It has to be smooth because you're really a tenderfoot. It has to be bright and have no glare; white, yet colorful; large, yet intimate; elegant, yet casual; contrived, and yet seem to have just happened. It isn't easy.

After much wringing of the hands, you decide on textured concrete—not ordinary textured concrete, of course, but colorful pebbles set in white cement and ground to a smooth–rough texture like terrazzo and sealed to bring out the color of the stones and prevent water from penetrating the surface. This sounds not too difficult. But you always find that there's something like a truck-driver's strike and they aren't hauling or dredging the particular stones you want for probably six months. This leads to many excursions—safaris, really—to distant places in search of tiny pebbles. You try all the sources. (I'm abbreviating. You *invent* sources.) And then one day you discover that some guy three miles from home has a mountain of marble, imported from Italy, in every conceivable color and a few that are inconceivable. This is fascinating. The only trouble is that these are not pebbles. They're not round. They're jagged pieces of marble—the right size, but jagged—so the guy tells you that for a slight extra charge, he can toss these in a mechanical tumbler and wear off the edges so they look just like the pebbles you were looking for in the first place. You embed these in the concrete in variegated colors, grind them smooth with a grinding machine, test them with your bare feet, apply the sealer to see what happens to the colors, look at them from a distance, look at them close by, test the surface with water for possible puddles. It all looks great—to everyone but the client. He discovers puddles where no one else can see them. He notices several areas where the pebbles are unevenly distributed or have too much of one color of where some of the pebbles have come loose from the concrete in the grinding process. You take the whole thing too lightly, so the client collects all the pebbles that have come loose and puts them in a basket, like an autumn harvest, for you to see. Several sections are intolerable. They're driving him mad. He can't sleep. His wife pleads with you. Eventually the offending sections are removed and replaced. The mason is in the doghouse. Law suits are threatened. "Experts" are called in. The client finds loose pebbles in the *new* concrete. By now *he's* an "expert"—a made expert. No one will come near the job—not even the other experts. After an appropriate time lapse, as with a death in the family, you make a courtesy call one bright morning, early, to catch the client before he takes off (for business). The pool and the paving are dazzling, glittering in the sunlight, smooth to the foot, textured to the eye, variegated in color, sensuous in form. The client is on his hands and knees, in the posture of prayer, but, in fact, gluing some recalcitrant pebbles back into place with a new adhesive he has discovered. After an exchange of condolences on a State Department level, he invites you to breakfast. After coffee, he decides he can live with it. It isn't easy.

You may discredit this as the birth of an American garden. (It's really a garden for the one who has everything—except a barbeque.) Of course, it fits neatly into the idea that most Europeans seem to still have about the way Americans live. It's certainly one kind of American garden. But I don't know what an American garden is. I'm sure that the same garden would turn out quite differently if it were done for a Frenchman in France or a German in Germany or a Japanese in Japan. (I did a garden in Germany, once—even went over there to design it on the site, and staked it out in the ground. I couldn't stay to supervise it, but I explained every stone and nuance in marvelous detail. There was a great deal of "Yah, yah" and "So? So?," which I mistook for communication, but when I saw photographs of the completed job, it was definitely German.) I'm sure the same garden done for a different American would be entirely different. I find myself completely tongue-tied when someone—particularly a European—asks me what an American garden is. It's something like asking what an American is. But the European usually puts a diabolical twist to the question, like the editor of a German garden magazine who once asked me to write an article about how Americans liked to *live* in their gardens. These assumptions about assumptions just slay me. I'm trying to figure out whether there is such a thing as an American garden, and the editor has a have-you-stopped-beating-your-wife question all ready for me. I don't know how Americans would like to live in the gardens that they haven't got, any more than I know whether they would beat their unborn children. I can only guess. I suppose they'd like to live in the gardens that they haven't got, in the way they'd like to live in a heaven that they haven't reached, and I'm sure that would be different for everyone.

In heaven (I'm guessing again), I presume that one man would like to have the largest flowers, another the most possessions, and still another the greatest peace of mind. Of course, we don't always get what we

want in gardens, as we do in heaven—that's probably because heaven is made by God, and gardens by landscape architects—but I do think that the kind of a garden one gets depends on the kind of image one has of oneself. In this respect, Americans are the same as Germans or Japanese, or any other people for that matter. The difference is in the way they see themselves—or do not see themselves—in nature. I doubt that average Americans see themselves in nature at all. They're way above that. Gardening is still big business (ranking ninth or tenth, I think), but this is seed catalogue and flowering bushes stuff—a sentimental and seasonal offering to the lost art of being with it. A new car or an extra bathroom carries more prestige in the average community than having a garden. Any real estate agent will tell you that a garden has nothing to do with resale value. The land can be tortured, the house disoriented, the living room a mausoleum (what a challenge to decorate) as long as it has the respectable foundation planting and other wall-to-wall stupidities. The American garden is not a garden for one who has everything. It's the illusion of one who is without it.

He has to be cheated—wants to be cheated—into some kind of "with it." Of course, he's a difficult customer. He's miserable. Isn't everybody? Besides that, he keeps saying he *likes* being miserable. Well, I don't know anyone who won't let him continue as long as he likes. Occasionally, however, you get someone who's miserable and admits he doesn't like it, but *has* to live with it. That can be fun. It happened to me once—the client who had everything wrong, and knew it. He'd just moved from the Bronx to Suburbia. I don't know why. The important thing was that he saw it fresh. I don't mean "fresh as a daisy." I mean "fresh," like something he'd never seen before. I don't think he'd ever been out of the Bronx, and Suburbia startled him. His new house had been placed by the builder (for reasons that only builders have) at a strange angle to everything else so that it looked as though it had been left there by a flood. It was obviously a three-bedroom box, but it was impossible to find the front door. It was a pink house, I remember, and had a sort of cancan gesture to the street, exposing the indecencies of its garbage pails and kitchen door without much lyric quality. The drive was long—circuitous, if you should happen to want to put the car in the garage—and the lot small and narrow. Access to anything was simply unavailable, except for the clandestine view of the neighbor's living room, which appeared with the immediacy of a spy center for a Hitchcock movie. As so often happens in these neighborly situations, the families were not speaking. Something about the kids, I think.

Yes, Suburbia really took him by surprise. He was a statistician. I don't think he'd ever seen a garden plan or a shovel. But he had amazing determination and a terrifying curiosity (from which my telephone ear

has never fully recovered), and he built himself—almost single-hand-
edly—a fine garden that made the situation seem almost reasonable. I
don't know how he did it. I think he was somehow startled into it. He
had that fresh, bewildered look that says things can't possibly be like
this, but they are. Something happened and I don't know what it was. It
was an image, I think. The way he saw himself. It's almost impossible to
describe because it wasn's a fixed thing but more like a process—like
growth—that produced his own image in nature and within the social
framework where each had existed only separately before. That's how
gardens are born.

PART II

Ah, Japan

YOU, Again

I have more definitions. You won't like them, but they're positively great: A Japanese garden is a garden made in Japan. A German garden is a garden made in Germany. A French garden is a garden made in France. A Spanish garden is a garden made in Spain. An American garden is a garden made by an American. And Greece *is* a garden, made in Greece. There's no such thing as a garden where it's people aren't. That's a *translation,* not a garden. And if you think that makes no difference, if you think there's something solid about a garden that can be raked back and forth over any soil, then you're being YOU again. You're standing outside, being superior—not part of it—and the game can't even begin, not with you.

I've seen you in those Japanese flower arrangement classes, and boy, it's sickening. Don't you realize that the Japanese have been doing this for a thousand years? Probably longer. It's a way of life for them. They give up kitchens—your idea of kitchens—for the tokonoma. Their whole house is designed around the tokonoma. Would you give up a kitchen—would you give up anything for a flower arrangement? Of course not. You want to cheat and you're terrible at it. You think you can have both. You think the Japanese will give a little—they'll see it your way, partly, like a good sport. Like YOU. But you don't know how stubborn they are. They're as stubborn as you are. But it's their game and they're inside it. They're with it. You're outside, with-out it.

Of course, you can have a real Japanese garden. All you have to do is be Japanese. But you wouldn't like that. They see things differently. And you see things they don't see. That may surprise you, but YOU see things they don't see and these things keep interfering and you won't give them up. YOU won't give up anything. That's the way you are. And the Japanese can't see it that way. And don't think that I think I've convinced you. If I had, you wouldn't be YOU. There is a way, however, and it's not as complicated as you think. It's not nearly complicated enough for YOU. All you have to do is go back to the beginning.

It used to bother me, bother me painfully—I mean the way pimples bother an adolescent—when people would call my gardens "Japanese." Of course, I knew it wasn't so. It couldn't be. I didn't know enough about Japanese gardens to do one. I had never seen a Japanese garden. But some lady in a hat who had just come back from Japan would always say, "It's just like being set down in the center of Japan," and I can't tell you how this used to bother me. I didn't realize then that she was really thinking about her hat and about what other people were thinking about her hat and she didn't know a damn about gardens anywhere, but she had to say something because she wanted people to notice that hat.

It doesn't bother me anymore. I just say, "Yes, and you'd be surprised how much the Japanese have learned from this garden," and that really floors them. Strangely enough, I learned this little trick from an American, Robert Frost. You'd be surprised what you can learn from Robert Frost. About gardens, too, and flower arrangement and even how to do them, and he never studied in Japan, either. But there's nothing you need to know that he didn't know from the beginning, and I guess that's why when this student asked him what he did when people read things into his poems that he had never intended—things that maybe weren't even there—he just said, "I accept them."

I think Frost would have done wonderful gardens. In fact, I think he *did* wonderful gardens and I'll bet he never read a how-to-do it in his life. I'm sure he never studied in Japan. You wouldn't think that anything like him could come out of Vermont. It's positively mysterious. But that's what I mean. I think it's just plain mysterious when one American, stuck way up in the woods of Vermont, can get it and a million others cannot—not even with all the special classes and the magazines and the garden books and sometimes years of study.

I don't pretend to understand the reason. I think it has something to do with words. Yes, with words, because we think in words. And with logic because we're trained in logic. I don't mean we have courses in logic like we have courses in flower arrangement. That would be different. Because then we would be as bad at logic as we are at flower arrangement. It would be a second or third or fourth language and we'd be terrible at it—the way the Japanese are—but we're good at logic. Terribly good at it. It's either/or for us, and nothing else. No nonsense. Two and two equals four, and that's that. Or take whatever other system you want to, and that's that. There's no in-between. Everything else is frustration. It's as if you were trying to teach a kid the alphabet—I said *the* alphabet, so naturally I mean our alphabet, the A B C one—and when you got up to K and started for L, the kid decided he'd like to have something between K and L. Then you'd have to explain that there was nothing between K and L. But if the kid kept insisting on something between, you'd have a problem.

Of course when YOU say "nothing" you mean nothing. But the kid hasn't been nearly so well indoctrinated as you. He might even think you mean NOTHING. And to him this might mean EVERYTHING, and he might be intrigued with the whole idea. But YOU will straighten him out. And pretty soon he will see that "nothing" means *nothing* and that's what lies between K and L and between everything that is not either/or and that's that. At least he will probably *say* so because YOU get mad so easily and you're bigger than he is.

Well, that's something of the way it is when YOU start dabbling in Japanese gardens, except that the Japanese are not kids and you don't appear quite so large to them. In fact, you don't come into it—into the game, I mean—because you're so "either K or L," and they leave you alone. Of course, even the way they leave you alone is different from the way YOU would leave anyone alone. You probably wouldn't get it. They might give you a set of tools of your own to play with. They might throw in some Japanese words that you can use back at the garden club. They might even let you teach them. (That's almost irresistible.) When you think you've convinced them that there's really nothing between K and L, then you're the real YOU—"very reasonable."

If you're a more or less percpetive YOU, you will probably begin to sense that something's wrong. But you're still YOU. So you will feel very strongly about it. If you feel strongly enough about it, you will become one of the professional Asiastics. You won't be able to give up much of the original "YOU," however. That's pretty basic. But you'll add some "THEM." You'll be seeing it both ways, and that's quite an achievement. If your field of interest is landscape, you'll do several things. You'll probably learn the language when you discover that it's more strange than it is difficult. You'll do it with a thoroughness and urgency that will astound the Japanese. The inexactness of it will annoy you, but only briefly, because you'll sense your superiority when you learn that the Japanese have to have something written in English or French, and then translated back into Japanese when they really need to "tie things down." Something legal, for instance. Finally, you'll be good-naturedly amused to find that the Japanese have blind spots in sound. Something like color blindness, but in sounds. It's like having *nothing* between K and Q, and that's quite different from the nothing between K and L. This makes their English at least as bad as your Japanese—probably worse, because these things are important in English—and there's kind of a democracy in that, and it makes you feel comfortable.

Another thing that this more or less perceptive YOU will do is take classes. Classes in flower arrangement—you can't get away from that —classes in Bonsai, perhaps, classes in landscape gardening, even Sumiye. You will very quickly discover that there's the right way, your way, the wrong way, and the Japanese way. The Japanese way will prevail as long as you remain in the classes. You will remain in the classes, of course, because you have integrity, determination, drive, honesty, curiosity, self-consciousness, and all the other virtues including a terrible sense of ignorance. It will take all of these virtues because the Japanese will ignore completely your most prized accomplishment—your individuality. You will learn "techniques." Japanese techniques. These are sometimes vague, and yet not so vague. Sometimes they're really symbols that become techniques. But by this time, you've grown used to the Japanese way with words and it doesn't make that much difference. You didn't realize before that the tortoise and the crane were the symbols of long life, but that's important. That's the way they see it. Every garden should have a tortoise and/or a crane, but not necessarily. A circle is symbol of the purity of mind if you see it that way, but it can also mean something else if you don't. Everything means something else. A round jug is the moon and with the gate and the branch you are told how to feel when you enter the house. You have to learn these things. They're very elusive, and yet not so elusive.

In effect, you will be learning another language—a landscape language, Japanese style. You will, of course, stumble around, off-balance. It's their language. And you will be amazed at how particular they can be about it—and yet not so particular, at the same time. But because you *are* perceptive, you will realize this is far from kid stuff. It *sounds* that way in the beginning, but it has levels. Some of them are pretty shallow, but it has no bottom. You can go as deep as you like and never reach bottom. You're not in the Bahamas playing around with quaint native lore—although you can do that, too, if that's your level—you're in over your head and not a life raft in sight.

Every once in a while you will notice out of the corner of your "mind" that something else is always present. You won't pay much attention to it. You know what nature is. If the truth could be told, it's a terrible bore. It's contrary. It's always *doing* something. And doing it at the wrong time. You can't trust it. There ought to be a way . . . a nature controller, perhaps. They're doing such wonderful things nowadays. That's the nice thing about back home. They keep nature where nature belongs. That must be another one of those blind spots of the Japanese. They don't seem to mind. In fact, they wallow in it—like sea life in the sea—when they could just as easily have a nice safe boat on the surface, like YOU.

I *said* they were stubborn. They're like those gaddamn fish in the sea. I don't know why you bother with them. If you're going to play fish, you're going to play it as the fishes do. If you don't you're going to look very silly just making like a fish. Logic will get you nowhere. You can see that. I never said you were stupid, just that you were YOU. You can see their blind spots. You've been to classes. You've got yourself in deeper than you ever thought possible. You didn't realize it, but you're becoming an authority. If you were an idiot, you'd write a book. But right now it's enough to just live in two worlds. I mean *outside* two worlds. You're not in the boat and you're not in the sea. The Japanese have begun to respect you. Why not? You "know" more about their world than they do. They just live it. And then with the "foreigners" you're really great. Boy, are you great. You should see yourself. You don't know any of the answers. You suspect there aren't any. That's western stuff. But you also know that the "foreigners" think that there *must* be answers. That's the way they are—just like you were a few years ago—they don't even suspect the no-answer bit, and boy, do YOU let them have it. You're a real pro.

In a way, I suppose you're entitled to hold court with the "foreigners." You're in a good position to see the over-all picture. You're outside of both. The Japanese can't do it because they find it as difficult to come outside as you find it to come in and the "foreigners" don't even know there is an "inside." YOU know there's both because now you're outside both. Something has happened to you. You're beginning to see things. On the one hand, it's like mingled voices in a foreign tongue where you occasionally hear sounds you think you can identify—like something in your own language—but they're not. You can make an awful fool of yourself when you answer as if they were. On the other hand, it's like listening, but not listening, to the babble of your own language in a foreign restaurant. It's painful because you can distinguish all the accents, where they come from. You can even see the kind of wallpaper and graduation exercises and Sunday afternoons. So you push it back to babble where its like a foreign tongue.

Ah, Japan   It's hard to say which is first to emerge as meaning when you listen to the Japanese landscape, especially when you speak with precise western logic and can't bear to listen to it anymore. The Japanese landscape has its own form of separateness. It's illusory, not immediate. You have to go to it. It isn't there. But sometimes it is there. They give you a tree and half a hill, and ask you to fill in the woods with imagination, or a bonsai and a stone, and ask you to see nature, or a dewdrop, and ask you to see the universe. It's nature painting, not a landscape. It represents something, it's never the thing itself. But what is the "thing"? Is is what YOU carry with you?

Banish the thought. The thing is what you're looking for. Only you don't know what it is. By now you have a thousand techniques. You have them all classified. Right in your notebook. There's the hill garden, the flat garden, the tea garden, and all the things that go in them. Stones. Always stones. But the stones have shapes and combinations, even a sex. You didn't know that before, but stones have a sex. It's symbolic, of course, but stones have a sex—if you see them that way. The Japanese do. And then there are the other things—the stone lanterns, pagodas, bridges, water basins—and you're an expert on all of them, as expert as you can be about anything that keeps floating around in so much symbolism and never holds still long enough so that you can pin it down. The Japanese eventually get it all pinned down, in some miraculous way, but they can't explain how. It isn't *this* way or *that* way, but somewhere in that infuriating in between. It's not so much tied down as suspended. In any event, it's held, and make no mistake about it, it's Japanese.

You haven't become Japanese, of course, but you have changed—noticeably. You've become a professional Asiatic, an outsider-in-between. This is serious. In the process of acquiring insights into the Japanese way, you have also acquired some of their outward characteristics. For one thing, you are more polite—and you haven't neglected the Japanese firmness under it. Now, we "foreigners" have to do things *your* way. You are patient with us, but firm—vague, too. We're not quite sure what we're supposed to do or say, and you won't tell us—can't tell us, perhaps—we're too either/or. But you're terribly polite about it. Nothing bothers you anymore. Almost nothing. If something does, you're too polite to show it. You forgive us—except in little ways we don't quite get and you won't tell us, can't tell us. We're just never *right*. We do it one way and you say, "Oh, well," and we do it the *other* way and you say, "Oh, well." There's not a decent "yes" or "no" left in you. And when we say something, you don't care if a trolley car is passing by. You're so close to the edge of something—just sitting there, immovable—I feel an irresistible urge to push you into whatever abyss

you're contemplating. I would, too, except that I always try to fight politeness with politeness. But sometimes I think you will eventually force me to reconsider the old YOU—that crazy, naive, logical, wordy, straight-thinking, inconsistent, definable, lovable YOU.

I don't know why, but professional Asiatics always seem to be saying that the Japanese have some kind of secret. Something that the old YOU wouldn't understand in a million years. The Japanese themselves aren't above this kind of promotion either, especially when you're so delightfully gullible. They love to play games. But I don't think they believe they have any secret. It's quite obvious to everyone that YOU haven't any secret, but that's quite different from saying that they have. It's just that their first language is NATURE, and yours is logic and words.

Getting behind a first language is difficult. There's no denying that. Particularly when the first language is so logical and the words form such a perfect pattern of their own. You try to get with nature by look-

59

ing through this pattern, but nature is on one side and YOU are on the other. Somehow, you have to get through this screen. You have to get between K and L. And that's very difficult because, as any properly indoctrinated third-grader will tell you, there's nothing there. NOTHING and EVERYTHING. But in *this* third grade, you have to throw away logic and words and start over. Don't worry about losing them. You can't. Probably not even long enough for an experiment. They've got YOU. They *are* YOU. You're identified with them so completely that you think everybody is YOU. You've been waiting for them to see your light. But it isn't either THEM *or* YOU. It's "IT." And "IT" is inside that in-between. YOU have to go there—not to Japan—if you want to do a garden. That's where nothing is. No rocks in words. No logical deductions. Just you and nothing so combined they might be called N-Y-O-U-T-H-I-N-G—which is different from either YOU or NOTHING just as water is different from hydrogen and oxygen. That is the beginning. That's where you begin yourself. That is the first language. And after that, the rest falls into place.

If you think this sounds crazy, let me be the first to agree with you. What game isn't? Yours? Be yourself. If you want to play, you have to get with the game. If you prefer to stand outside and watch and analyze and be dignified and superior, go ahead. Who cares? That's the way YOU are. But if you want to play, jump in. And for God's sake, stop rocking back and forth on that east-west precipice. You make me nervous. Now, leave all that logical junk of yours right where it is and JUMP. Go ahead. JUMP.

You see. It wasn't so bad. But boy, you looked terrible back there. That logical screen of yours is more like a cage than a screen when you see it from here. It has something though. A kind of overall, God-like view. It has nothing to do with God, of course. It's a bunch of people acting like God—seeing the overall view—or rather, making the overall view what they see and then saying "That's IT." Well, of course it is—for them. But you can see many things from here you couldn't see outside. I should say you can be many things. You can see outside, better than before. You know things, too. You know the Japanese, for instance, and you don't have to take any classes in it either because they're with it and you're with it, too. You're speaking the same language, the first language, and it hasn't any words.

I don't mean that you've become Japanese or anything like that. That's what the professional Asiatics are trying to do. I just mean that you speak the same language and that doesn't make you any more like the Japanese than speaking English made you like Shakespeare. And it's not going to help you to do "Japanese" gardens. If you want to do Japanese gardens, you'd better go back on the cliff and start teetering again, and make like a Japanese. Why you ever wanted to "do" *anybody* else's gardens second-hand, I can't imagine. Yes, I can, too. You thought there was a secret. A mysterious brew that makes pumpkins into gardens. Well, there isn't.

When and Where?

I once asked a Japanese architect how long he thought it would take an American, living in Japan, to really understand the Japanese way—the Japanese thinking, the Japanese culture. He was a serious person, and thought about his answer a long time—so long that I was ready to change the subject—and then he said, "About six hundred years." The magazines have no difficulty doing it in a few months. And the Japanese will help them. They're like that. They have a wonderful sense of humor.

The magazines send their scouts and photographers. In a few months they become authorities on everything Japanese—gardens, food, customs, manners, theatre, and the whole panorama of Japanese life. Enough to keep the magazine going for a year. I think it's remarkable. And it's "very reasonable." Why not? What's the mystery? (Well, the mystery is still YOU.) But after a while, I get a little sick of having the west made to appear idiotic because it's "reasonable." Even that has some advantages—advantages that the Japanese don't readily grasp because they are alogical. As a race, they are alogical. And that's at least one "reason" why we don't understand them or their gardens and probably never will. Certainly not in a few months. It takes longer than that to understand that we *don't* understand them. I have to give the magazines credit for proving that.

Of course, our way is just as mysterious to the Japanese. That's even more difficult for us to believe. We're so "straightforward" and "simple" that *anyone* can understand *us*. Not the Japanese. You should see what they come up with when they think they're doing "western style." It's as hilarious as our attempts at Japanese gardens, only we don't realize how hilarious that is. It's too bad. We miss a great joke all around. Neither we nor the Japanese seem to realize that there are times to dissect a flower with a scalpel and there are times to get inside it like a Buddha. It's as ridiculous to be alogical about how to get to the grocery store as it is to be logical about experiencing revelation. In this sense, I suppose the West has made its contribution, but like the East, it sees its contribution as the whole thing. Of course, it's idiotic to be just "reasonable," but it isn't exactly wisdom to be without reason.

Now, I feel free to compare gardens. This will be difficult for me because I don't have the magazine gift of seeing out of context—of seeing "gardens" as one thing and the people they come from as another. I tend to look at little things, anyway. I don't look at "GARDENS." I look at the people, how they walk. You'd be surprised what you can tell about their gardens from the way the people walk—the way they do anything—serve the table, drive a car, greet each other, look at a child. It makes no difference so long as you find the trait and don't mistake it for the act.

It doesn't hurt to read a book or look at gardens. But you have to be careful. There are a lot of things between you and them. Authors are cagey, I know, and gardens, are, too, I suspect. But people aren't thinking about the way they walk, or the why about it. In Spain, it isn't walking at all. It's more like a dance. It's a kind of a dance just to walk down the street and they're very skillful at it. They hardly ever touch each other, even when the street is crowded. There are all sorts of signals going on between them, telling each other which way they're going and after a while you catch on to the signals and hardly ever bump into anyone even if you're not very skillful—because they are—and it's like having a good dance partner if you know how to follow.

In Greece, it's completely different. They have different signals because they're doing something different. They're "companioning." It's almost impossible to walk alone, or do anything alone, in Greece because they have this thing they call "companioning." You may start out alone, but before you know it you're walking with someone and soon there are three and then five or more. They form like molecules and then separate again in new combinations. I don't know why. It's a trait. A game, I guess. Nobody tells anyone what to do. It just happens if you let it. The same thing doesn't happen in America or in England or in Spain or in Japan, but it happens in Greece. And the landscapes are like that in Greece—not private yards and terraces and gardens like we have—but the whole thing is a garden for everybody. The town or village is a terrace, or a lot of terraces. They belong to everyone, I guess, because anyone can come out and sit around, but he won't be alone. He'll be "companioning" because the Greeks are like that and they make their landscapes like that.

The Greek landscape isn't much like the Italian landscape. The Italians don't walk the same way. They have something in common perhaps, but they don't think the way they do in Greece. You give an Italian a piece of ground and he'll immediately make it into a "square"—a living room—not the dead, mausoleum type to show who he is, but a real "living" room. He uses it that way and I don't think it's because he read in a book or a magazine that that's the way you're supposed to use it. It's because he's Italian and that's the way you use a living room if you're an Italian. He'll even show you how to use his living room. He won't say anything or give you a book of instructions, but there'll be a million signals flashing around, telling you how to act, and pretty soon you'll know how to use his living room. But please don't take his living room home. Americans won't get the signals because the signals won't *be* there and they'll be too busy with their own. They'll make it into a parking lot with drugstores all around.

I'm not going to ask you not to take Japanese gardens home because you will, anyway. They're in vogue right now, with all the books and magazines hammering away at them, but I think you ought to first watch the way the Japanese walk. It's different from anybody—especially YOU. You're self-conscious, but there's something *obtrusive* about the Japanese. Yes, obtrusive. They're terribly polite and all that, but there's something obtrusive about the way they walk, about the way they do everything. At least it seems obtrusive to me because I'm an American, right on the edge of your petri dish, looking over the side, and from there it looks obtrusive.

That's partly because I don't play the game properly, I know, but there are some things you can see better from the edge than you can see from either side. You have to respond completely or you can't get into the game. I respond completely, but with reservations, and that keeps me out. I'm almost exactly on the fifty-yard line though, and that's a pretty good spot for viewing. And from there, I shouldn't really mention the Japanese obtrusiveness first. It's important, but it isn't first. You first have to see it the way they see it and that's difficult to do. It's idiotic to try. I wouldn't even begin except that I know an enigma when I see one, and if there's one thing you can depend on about an enigma, it's that whatever you say about it will be true. That's what an enigma is. Something you can talk about forever and you'll always be "right," even when you're "wrong," and the other fellow will always be "wrong" even though he's the "rightest" guy I know. That's why there's so much talk about Japanese gardens.

You think the Japanese are shy? Well, you're "wrong." Don't be fooled by that fan you think they're hiding behind. They're not hiding behind it, they're looking through it. They're curious, not shy, but they want to appear *delicately* curious, and when you think it's shyness, you've lost the first round of the game right there. This is a fast game, so pay attention from now on. Don't forget that fan, either. It's part of their gardens. You're always looking through something, seeing it their way. It's very delicate.

If you look through a fan and you're curious at the same time, you get even more curious because you don't see it all at once. If you want to see it all at once, if you want to "dissect" it—find out what makes it tick—get a clock and take it apart, but don't fool with Japanese gardens. At any rate, don't ask the Japanese. They don't know. It just ticks—for them—because they're "ticky." The question is how they got that way.

In each culture, there are certain things that catch on—become permanent parts of it—and other things which are just fads or novelties—temporary. The things which catch on permanently suit the basic traits of the people and nothing else will do. You never see the living room "square" evolve spontaneously in Japan, as you do in Italy. When it happens, it's "thought out," and usually by someone else. Not the Japanese. It doesn't suit the Japanese character. They prefer what we call "alleys," where you can never find your way. You mope around until you come upon whatever you're headed for. They can't find their way, either, but it doesn't make any difference. They're alogical, and it suits them. I could make a diagram—but it isn't like a diagram. It's nothing like a diagram. That's logical. And I don't think you can understand something that's alogical by making up a logical explanation or a diagram. It's formless. It has depths—many layers in depth—it meanders around and finally gets settled, somehow, but there's no logical explanation because the people aren't that way.

That's why I think you get much further by just watching the way they walk. It isn't like anyone in Europe or America or even Asia, as far as I know. Even when they wear western shoes, they walk in a kind of scuffle as though they were trying to keep their slippers on. The body has sort of "tipsy" motions like wild ducks uncertain about which is north and which is south. They can have a whole street to walk on, and when you see them coming you're certain they're going to bump into you. You think they don't see you. They don't look at you, but they know you're there all right because they always miss you. In some miraculous way, they always miss you, but the important thing is that you know they were there and passed you because they missed you. That's what I mean by "obtrusive." It's the same thing children have when they want to get attention only it's more clever than that. It's a developed trait. And don't be fooled when it isn't there—when they're *unobtrusive*—because that's part of the same thing, only skillfully trained. It's much cleverer than children. It's like children who keep on being children, but don't forget to grow up, either.

Of course, this is in only one trait—perhaps not the most important—but it comes out in gardens. They arrange those damned stones so you walk in a certain way—their way—or else you're a slob or you fall in the water. You're directed. You don't just stroll around. They call it "strolling," but it isn't. It's part of the "treatment"—the discipline, the training—in how to walk unobtrusively. But it's obtrusive, too. You're told where to go and what to do by every stone and branch in the place, and I don't think this is any accident. It isn't the German kind of discipline, either. That's different. The Germans often think it's the same, but they have difficulty in seeing themselves. The two meet, in the briefest way imaginable, because they're both disciplines. They meet the way a hummingbird approaches a flower and then is off again.

One thing I "miss" in Japanese gardens—either through lack of perception or because it isn't there—is the sense of roundness, particularly the "happened" roundness. I'm not talking about roundness in the sense of curves or spheres. I'm talking about roundness in the western sense of sculpture. The Japanese garden has modulation and depth, but it is essentially a pictorial experience like a painting—without inness, the state of being *in* something. You are "at" it. And the immediacy of getting "in" is an additional step of projection which is philosophical or psychological rather than physical. Physically, they're flat. Pictures. Many pictures–often contrived. Usually contrived, in fact. You have to go to them, and see them in a certain way—the Japanese way —and that is as a painting. Nature painting. There is even one garden so contrived that it's whole point builds up to the moment when you wash your hands at the stone basin—a symbolic gesture of cleansing the mind—and at that moment and in that position only, you see the view, the "Ah" of enlightenment.

This is far more than "charming." It is at once a complete identity with nature and the result of a thousand years or more of a philosophic attitude. It is the Japanese way of involvement with nature. It is not arrived at through any logic or plan. It is there, and this is the way they reveal it. I doubt very much that they know how it is done. Or rather, they "know" how it is done, but they can't "describe" how it is done to the satisfaction of the western mind. Neither can I. It just "happens" that way, if you're Japanese. You are not. And unless you become Japanese, it will "happen" in your garden—if it happens at all—in a different way, *your* way.

It doesn't *always* happen in Japanese gardens. Far from it. There are many levels—some more profound and many many less so. In the great between, many things happen. They don't just "happen," either. They "come out" of the Japanese way of seeing things. There are often "brilliant passages," as they might be described if you were discussing paintings—a reworking of nature to make it more "natural" than nature, more comprehensible, less confusing—and there's a great deal of hobbling over stones to get a look at these "pictures" or "passages" in the total scene, peeking through fan-like "obstructions" which are really visual aids of a pretty obvious sort. One garden has something like a hundred and eight "pictures," each with its "viewing" stone. I don't get much "enlightenment" out of this. I get a little tired, and annoyed at being marched up the hill to look at a "picture" and then marched down again. The spaces between are often nothing more than boy scout paths for nature study. They're sort of leftover parts between the "pictures." You're on your own to scramble around as best you can. This surprises me because the Japanese are often so good at "making the connection," but it's part of the enigma and the Japanese blind spot, from the western point of view, in missing the gestaldt.

From the western point of view, all this is terribly disorganized, and at the same time it has an attractiveness that can't be ignored. People are not "important." That hurts. The Japanese wouldn't understand this because the people are "part" of it. What are you talking about, "important?" The circulation is "irrational," devious, up and down. (Now you're using logic, and the ear is still deaf.) They *contrive* to set up "pictures." Doesn't everyone? They "suggest" the total experience with a symbolic tree, a symbolic stone, and symbolic water, as in a painting, and that's cheating. Where is "it?" Well, it's all there—if you're Japanese.

Of course, this is not always done well. The western visitor gets the "guided" tour—the Japanese idea of what he wants to see—and this invariably leaves out the best and the worst. The Japanese don't evaluate their gardens or anything else with such polarity. That's western thinking. They do like to please, but that's not so important, either, if you want to be stubborn about it. They'd like you to feel good, but they're not going to argue. They don't have the words or the beautiful partitions of thought where "right" is right and "wrong" is wrong. It's just what it is. But you're going to see it the Japanese way. You're never actually pushed. The Japanese are too courteous for that, but you can often feel the iron hand beneath their velvet glove.

The Japanese "argument" isn't logical. It's more in the nature of "getting you in the mood." The effort to do this is endless. Sometimes it's subtle, and sometimes it's not so subtle. It ranges from the sublime "Ah" of enlightenment at the washing basin to definite instructions. "This is where you have to enjoy the garden." In between there is often a great deal of hocus-pocus which the American wouldn't tolerate for a moment at home, but in Japan he is a complete sucker for the "treatment," and the Japanese are experts at giving it. Every stone has its name. There's the "worshiping" stone, the "guardian" stone, the "removing-shoes" stone, and a thousand other "stones" in various patterns or arrangements, which also have enchanting names like "seagull" and "wild duck" wherein the stone is no longer a stone, but a metaphor. The westerner loves this. It's back in the comfortable realm of words again where things are not what they are. They're words. And if the westerner likes words, the Japanese are not going to be so inhospitable as to deprive him of them. If you don't like one word, he will always have a more acceptable one handy. It's part of the "treatment." The important thing is to get you "in the mood" so you leave that awful YOU at the door with your shoes and saber so you can begin to see things.

But it's impossible to talk about Japanese gardens as if they were a "thing." We're always doing that. It's necessary to make them understandable to the western mind. Everything is a "thing" to be dissected and classified, "tied down" and forgotten. This "continuing" business is a nuisance. You never know where you are. Well, continuing with this particular "nothing," it's the essence of its myopic groping—like the scuffling of the Japanese walk—that it can't be "tied down." "That's a 'problem'," as the Japanese are fond of saying. And part of the "problem" is that Japanese gardens are by no means conveniently at their highest level today in order to coincide with the sudden American interest in them. That may be "unthoughtful" of Japanese gardens, but they are what they are.

The Japanese are capable of reversals in attitude—so sudden that it leaves the western mind gasping—but they don't become un-Japanese because of this. This *is* Japanese. They never were motivated by principles, as the west is. The reversals are not reversals at all in our sense. They are simply another way of looking at it, but the eyes are still Japanese. And being "still Japanese" means that they are bound by tradition in a way we cannot conceive. There's nothing to "give up," as we would think, no "starting over" because it's a "continuing" rather than a "fixed" thing as YOU, with your principles, always thought. The Japanese can't step outside of nature and view it as a "thing to dissect," as we do.

So how do you cope with the present situation if you are Japanese? The Japanese haven't found the answer in their gardens. Not yet. When they depart from their framework—their tradition, if you like—they go wild. Not attractively wild, just wild—like a flying fish that must by its nature and gravity return to the water. It's a dilemma. How are the Japanese to get outside of nature while remaining "in?" "That's a problem," they say. But how is the west to get back "in" nature while remaining "out"? That *is* a problem.

Having said all this, I'm going to be outrageous and un-Presbyterian enough to say that there's not a word of truth in it. And YOU almost fell for it! I was almost "making sense." Well, now you know you can't "trust" me. What I said was the way I see it, all right, but I'm not looking for "the truth." YOU are. I don't care whether it's true or not. It makes no difference. Don't you see that? The purpose is not to describe Japanese gardens so they won't come loose. There is no "truth." It's just in the way you see it. If you see it, it's true. If you don't, it doesn't exist. I could just as well have used X and Y, but you're so enamored with Japanese gardens that you won't listen to anything else. Besides, I'm saving X and Y for my own gardens. That's where X and Y are needed because YOU think you know American gardens so well that you won't listen if you think I *am* talking about them. See how YOU are?

You won't get the "truth" from the Japanese, either. They'll say anything they feel is expected of them. From their point of view, that's only common courtesy—not a "lie," and it's not a "sin" to tell one, anyway. All those stories the Japanese give out about their gardens couldn't possibly be "true." They're not exactly a "lie," either. I know because I *do* gardens. I live gardens. And sometimes when I hear what people say about my own, I could *die* gardens. It's unbelievable the things that people will read into an innocent little garden. That's the difference between a connoisseur and the person who actually does something. The connoisseur has to "explain" it or be unhappy. Well, nobody wants to see a connoisseur unhappy, so nobody says anything, and that's how a lot of stories grow up around a garden or anything you do because people keep repeating these stories and they never get them quite straight and, by the time they're as old as the Japanese stories about their gardens, there are so many of them that you can pick and choose any one you like and then everyone's as happy as a connoisseur because it's all pinned down. Well, it isn't.

You can't take gardens out of the people and "explain" them away. It's murder. You're killing the goose again instead of just being thankful that it lays the golden egg. You can take the basic traits of a people like the Japanese—the way they see things—and after enough discipline and training and "living it," you might turn these traits and way of seeing things into a Ryoanji Temple garden, but you can't bring "it" back to Brooklyn five hundred years later—or five minutes later, for that matter—that is, you can't bring it back alive. I don't care if it's "identical"—or more so. Even if it's less so or nearly so, it's about as alive as one of those dinosaurs in the Museum of Natural History, and if you think the Ryoanji Temple garden in Brooklyn is the "same thing," or ever could be the same thing, as the one in Kyoto, then I suggest that the next time you feel like eating a plum, you look at a picture of someone eating a plum instead. It will be the same thing.

The Ryoanji Temple garden in Kyoto isn't even the "same thing" in Kyoto that it once was. It's a museum piece. And I have no objection to museum pieces either in Kyoto or in Brooklyn. What bothers me is that YOU go around thinking its "real," and won't even look at what *is* real. You think there's some sort of secret—some magical something— locked up in the Ryoanji Temple garden, if you can only "capture" it. Well, in a way, you're right again. You're always "right." There *is* a magic secret locked up in the Ryoanji Temple garden. But for Buddha's sake, stop talking about "capturing" it. You make me think of chain gangs and fugitives and Javert wallowing through the sewers of Paris because somebody wanted a loaf of bread. If you want to "have" a Ryoanji Temple, you're going about it in the wrong way. Relax.

If you want anything like the Ryoanji Temple garden, you first have to "get with" some of the "what" through which it first "became." I know YOU don't like that kind of language, but if you think I'm going to fall for yours, and use words like "conditions" and "influences" and "effects," you're not as bright as I think you are. We'd be right back at the word game and in the middle of a wonderful argument and forget all about the Ryoanji Temple or any other garden because we'd be so busy setting the words in order that that would be quite enough, and what was it we were talking about, anyway? The point is that the Ryoanji Temple or any other garden never happened in a void—certainly not what YOU mean by void—and you can't reproduce it in *another* void. It isn't a question of "capturing" some abstract "principles of design," and putting them in a cage. Where is the "what"? The monks who brought the Ryoanji Temple garden into being probably never heard of your "principles." Couldn't have. That's a western invention. They did have a lot of "what," though, and it came out in their garden. The stones and sand and the climate that made the moss and the monks and the way they were—the way they saw things—and where they were and when, are all the same thing. When you take out the stones and sand, you have the stones and sand and YOU.

71

But let's leave the Ryoanji Temple out of this. That's for Brooklyn. You just want a plain old Japanese garden, and if you want it, I think you should have it by all means. You may even deserve it, and I'll be glad to tell you how to get it. First, let the Japanese do it for you. Don't YOU go fumbling around. This is their game, and they have the knowhow. This particular kind of obtrusiveness doesn't come naturally to Americans. The Japanese will do it just as they would at home—within the limitations of our local materials—because they don't know you or your neighbors or the situation or the American way. They'll feel entirely free on that score. Of course, the rocks won't be exactly "right" and the sand will be a little off-color. The Japanese are very particular about these things, but they also like to please, so you can handle them. If you're a perfectionist, you can send to Japan for the right sand and stones at the same time you send for the lanterns and other ornaments you will need. You can trust the water here and you can find enough appropriate plants, which have already been brought over by someone else. In short, it isn't too difficult to get a "real Japanese garden" in America, and with a Japanese gardener from Japan, you can probably "keep" it that way for some time.

Now you've got the thing. It's really kind of a special thing. When the Japanese garden-maker saw your house, he was no doubt very surprised, and suggested putting the garden as far away from it as possible. That's no handicap in Japan. A garden is often something you "go" to to renew your spirit. If you were smart, you followed his advice, even if he did call it a suggestion. Aside from the architectural problem of relating a Japanese garden to a western house, if you get it close, you will be tempted to use it. If you get it too close, you will *have* to use it. And naturally, having gone to all the trouble, you will want to use it properly—particularly at first.

Well, first let's see just how Japanese you want to be. I don't know. Maybe you've learned the rudiments of the tea ceremony. Most Japanese don't know it, and the few who do get a little nervous at the austerity of these occasions, but maybe you have the "drive." I don't know. But if you undertake anything like the team ceremony, I hope you remember when you greet your guests at the gate to the inner garden and after they have symbolically washed their minds at the stone basin—to be sure they leave their samurai weapons on the rack because you're going to be a terrible bore in America if you ask people to play Japanese seriously—to take their shoes off all the time and wear kimonos and all that—and I think you'll find that weapon rack a handy gadget.

And it isn't just special guests on special occasions. Maybe your guests like to squat in a four-and-a-half-mat teahouse and admire your pottery without conversation—it's considered enough just to watch the skill with which you perform the ceremony—but a lot of Americans don't get the point. There's grandmother, for instance, on Sunday afternoons. She'd never understand what you were getting at. She'd think you didn't like her any more. And your neighbors. They'd be rough on you too. They'd think you were putting on. They'd be right, of course, and since you're a reasonable person, you'd start making compromises. Little ones, at first. The wooden shoes have *got* to go. Kimonos, too. And you don't care what the Japanese gardener says, you want a place to sit down, and not one of those worshiping stones, either.

It's all very well for the Japanese to go hobbling around over those rocks, peeping at little pictures through natural peepholes. It was even fun in Japan. But in America, it's strictly for kibitzers. The sidewalk type. YOU want comfort, and I mean western-style comfort. Let them bring the view to your easy chair. You want to loll, and gossip, and watch those damned kids. And let them take out some of those rocks while they're at it to make space. And that teahouse! Was *that* a flop! Boy! Nobody understands the tea ceremony in this country. Lucky you didn't have to tear the house down to get Mrs. McGillicuddy's legs uncrossed, and everybody talked and talked . . . and it was so beautiful in Japan. . . .

But perhaps I've missed your whole point of view. You don't want a "teahouse" and all that. Well, what is it? An imitation? No, I'm *not* being impossible. I'm trying to find out. What do you want to do in this "Japanese" garden? Meditate? That's what the Japanese do. Some of them. You *do*? About what? The fullness of the Void? C'mon. OK, let's skip that. You don't want just the trimmings, do you? . . . Because. . . . An "*adaptation*"! I see. A western garden with Japanese fringe on top. Oh, I know it isn't that. Not exactly. It's a Japanese garden after the invasion. The sack of Japan, if you'll forgive my poetic license. Well, that's what you've got now that you've taken out the rocks and brought the view to YOU, and all your other little touches. They call this the "influence." I don't know whose on who, but you got it the hard way.

Why don't you take off that *mental* kimono? It looks silly. This isn't a masquerade. Or is it? You don't fool anyone, anyway. Not me or the Japanese or the neighbors, even grandmother. You can't even fool yourself indefinitely. I don't care what you put on, everybody will know you. Why don't you start there? With YOU? That's where you always end up, anyway. You do. Every time. So why not start there? First, I suggest you give a nice cocktail party. There's a reason for that. A "symbolic" reason. . . . Yes, they will. Most of them will come. They understand. They're just like YOU. Even Mrs. McGillicuddy. She won't trust you, but she'll come. She's too curious to stay away. Boy, she is curious, too, isn't she? I wouldn't even ask her to sit down if I were you. I'd play it cool.

Remember, the whole point is to wash your mind, get rid of that mangy kimono. It's symbolic. You start at the end—at YOU—which is really the beginning.

I almost forgot. I intended to give you some how-to-do-it hints on Japanese gardens. I took a course, you know. (From the same guy who brought the Ryoanji Temple garden back to Brooklyn.) I took the course right in Japan, and I have copious notes so I know what I'm talking about. I always take copious notes. When I first went to college, my dear Aunt Matilda (maiden) gave me a large notebook and told me to write down everything the professors said so I'd always have my education. I've always followed that advice. So I have copious notes.

I think I'll sell them to a magazine. The ones about Japanese gardens, I mean. (I'm sure the magazines have their own notes from college. Anyway, I think I can sell the college ones back to the professors if that isn't blackmail.) This same professor—the one who brought Ryoanji to Brooklyn—put out a pamphlet called *Japanese Gardens for California*. I don't think he likes California as much as Japan, but getting that pamphlet out sort of stole my thunder. However, I still have my notes and there's a lot more in them than there is in the pamphlet—any pamphlet, really. They tell you exactly how to do it. Exactly. Whether you want a "flat garden" (that's one without a hill or a pond) or a "hill garden." If you want a hill garden, you can have three kinds: *So, Gyo,* or *Shin* (rough type, intermediate type, or elaborated type).

On analysis of my notes, I find that they all have several things in common. In the stone line, they all have a "guardian" stone, a "perfect view" stone, a "seat of honor" stone, a "pedestal" stone, a "moon shadow" stone, a "worshiping" stone, a "waiting" stone. I assume, therefore, that these stones are "essential." Also the "principle" tree and the "tree of the evening sun" and the "tree of solitude" are found in all three types of hill gardens. The *So* type, for all it's "roughness," has a "hill" stone and a "label" stone, which neither of the others share. The *Gyo* type shares a "cliff" stone, "cave" stone, and a "cascade screening" tree with the *Shin* type, but has a "bridge" stone, a "distance" stone and two "cascade" stones all to itself. This is compensated for in the *Shin* type by a "view-perfecting" tree, a "tree of distance," and a "stretching" pine tree. It also has other features—a "near mountain," "companion mountain," "mountain spur," "near hill," and "distant peak"—which are called for in neither *So* nor *Gyo*, but I think it's most unique feature, and so appropriate to the *Shin* (elaborated) type, is something called an "idling" stone: neither *So* nor *Gyo* have this.

This is a very western analysis, of course. The way all this information was presented to me was much more mixed up. I had to find out for myself that these three types of hill gardens had things in common. The professor was very surprised. He'd never thought of it that way. And he won't think of it that way again, I'm sure. It just isn't Japanese. They don't "get" our classifications. They don't see what we're driving at. Even in something as simple as a menu for a western style meal, they get terribly confused. They can't make everything fit in, ending up with a number of items left over which they look at in surprise and label "other things" or simply "others."

Well, I've taken the trouble to "straighten out" the hill garden menu simply because I *am* western, but that's as far as I'll go. I'm turning it over to you—complete with diagrams for layout, rock arrangements, and "types of waterfalls"—so that you can choose your own dish. Just to keep the Japanese flavor, I'm adding an item which I found in my notes. Let's call it one of the "others." It's the exact measurements of the ten most important stones in the Ryoanji Temple garden (late of Brooklyn) with an appeal to finders to please write. (I wouldn't do it. With "secrets" like this you, too, can have a Ryoanji Temple garden in your own backyard.)

I have a word of warning to the hasty. Take it easy. Your neighbors will sooner or later find out the hill gardens shown here are what is known as "stereotypes." That's a dirty word in English, but not in Japanese. Even so, you should proceed with caution. There may be "other things" in a Japanese garden not included here. There certainly are "others"—boating-pond gardens, stroll pond gardens, viewing pond gardens, flat gardens, tea ceremony gardens (we've discussed that), "Zen-style" gardens, felicitous gardens (these have to do with wishing you "long life" and "lucky ideas" via stone and plant arrangements), dry pond gardens, condensed scenery gardens, "borrowed" scenery gardens (makes the distant view look as though you owned it), and "contemporary" gardens (quotes are mine). I haven's space to go into all these here, but you can borrow my notes any time. They're copious.

There is one strange thing about places that I don't understand at all: I can never seem to separate them from the people. I don't mean the people the way Carl Sandburg does when he says, "The People, Yes." That seems to me almost too "good" to be true. It's almost the same thing as "The People, No," if you want to look at it that way. I mean just the people who inhabit the place. "Yes" and "no" haven't much to do with it. They just *are* and the place *is* and there's no way of separating them. Absolutely no way. Not if they're the people of the place.

There's only one place that confuses me. That's Colorado. I'd like to do a garden there, but I can't seem to bring the place and the people together. I've only been in Colorado a couple of times. I can hardly remember it because it was either between train stops or I was just driving through, but it had something for me and it wasn't the people.

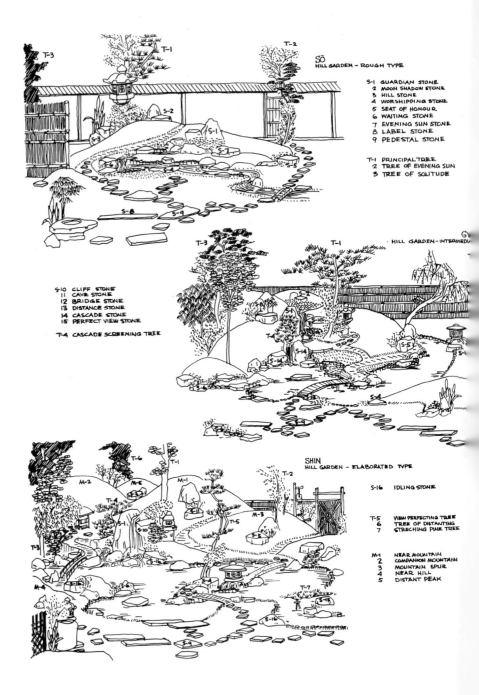

SŌ
HILL GARDEN - ROUGH TYPE

S-1 GUARDIAN STONE
2 MOON SHADOW STONE
3 HILL STONE
4 WORSHIPPING STONE
5 SEAT OF HONOUR
6 WAITING STONE
7 EVENING SUN STONE
8 LABEL STONE
9 PEDESTAL STONE

T-1 PRINCIPAL TREE
2 TREE OF EVENING SUN
3 TREE OF SOLITUDE

HILL GARDEN - INTERMEDIA

S-10 CLIFF STONE
11 CAVE STONE
12 BRIDGE STONE
13 DISTANCE STONE
14 CASCADE STONE
15 PERFECT VIEW STONE

T-4 CASCADE SCREENING TREE

SHIN
HILL GARDEN - ELABORATED TYPE

S-16 IDLING STONE

T-5 VIEW PERFECTING TREE
6 TREE OF DISTANTING
7 STREICHING PINE TREE

M-1 NEAR MOUNTAIN
2 COMPANION MOUNTAIN
3 MOUNTAIN SPUR
4 NEAR HILL
5 DISTANT PEAK

Maybe it was, but if it was, it was the ancient tribes, not the present inhabitants. But there was something about the colors that made it a very real something. It was blue. That's a crazy thing to say because nothing is blue. If Colorado were blue, you could get it in a paint can.

WATER FALLS

THREAD-FALLING (SHIRAITO)

RIGHT AND LEFT-FALLING (NIGIOCHI, HIDARIOCHI)

SIDE-FALLING (KATAOCHI)

FOLDING-FALLING (KASANEOCHI)

FRONT FALLING (MAEOCHI)

STEPPED-FALLING (DANOCHI)

LEAPING FALLING (HISEN)

WIDE-FALLING (HABAHIRO)

HEAVEN-FALLING (AMOCCHI NO TAKI)

LINEN-FALLING (NUNOBIKI)

GARDEN MENU

(JAPANESE STYLE)

ROCK FORMATIONS

SHOWN HERE ARE THE FIVE FUNDAMENTAL SHAPES OF NATURAL ROCKS OF PROPER COMBINATIONS OF 2,3,5,+7

BASIC FORM 1+2 "RECLINING, 3,4,+5 ARE "STANDING"

2 COMBINATION

3 COMBINATION

5 COMBINATION

7 COMBINATION

OTHERS

THE TEN MOST IMPORTANT STONES IN THE GARDEN OF THE RYOANJI TEMPLE, KYOTO. THE BROOKLYN BOTANIC GARDEN IS NOW SEEKING NEAR-DUPLICATES OF THESE STONES FOR ITS REPLICA OF THE RYOANJI GARDEN, FINDERS PLEASE WRITE: DIRECTOR'S OFFICE BROOKLYN BOTANIC GARDEN BROOKLYN 25, N.Y.

But Colorado was blue and that was so much a part of the place that I'd like to do a garden there; I don't know why.

In other places, the people are like the color in Colorado. It's something you can't take out of the place. For instance, there's an island off

77

the coast of Maine, which everyone says is just like one of the Greek islands. I can see exactly what they mean. It is and it isn't. Physically, it has many of the same characteristics. You could photograph it that way, and you'd never be able to tell whether it was part of Greece or not. But for me, it's New England and could never be anything else any more than Greece could ever become New England. Greece and New England. Boy!

Another place I'd like to do a garden, if it isn't already one, is Ireland. They don't seem to have any "gardens"—not by the magazine definitions. You see how you have to say, "they don't"? You could never say "it doesn't," because you could never take the Irish out of Ireland, no matter what you did or how far you took them, but I'd like to let a garden happen there. You could never "do" a garden in Ireland. You'd have to let it happen. And that's no different from Greece. Only a magazine would try to "do" a garden in Greece; the editors wouldn't see it already is one. For my own part, in Greece, I'd just get myself a pad and let early-born, rosy-fingered dawn "do" what it always has been doing.

It's different in Japan. The Japanese have to make gardens in Japan. They can't stop themselves. That's the way they are. But I wouldn't want to make a garden in Japan. I've had the opportunity, too, but I wouldn't want to do it. They'd love to see what a westerner would do with a garden in Japan, and sometimes I feel like showing them. I felt like that particularly before I ever went to Japan and had just seen the photographs and the books. The photographs and the books and what they say still confuses me about Japan. I thought I had a pretty good idea before I went there. What I didn't realize was that in all my life I'd never met a single Japanese. Even if I had met some in this country, I realize now it wouldn't have made any difference. We're too overpowering and they're too polite. We don't even see them, and they have that wonderful sense of humor. Of course, you could travel in Japan forever, and never see the Japanese. A lot of people do. I said *see*—not "look at" or "try to understand." Please don't try to understand. Westerners are always trying to "understand." There's nothing to understand. It just is what it is, and when and where. Do you understand a peony?

PART III

Here and Now

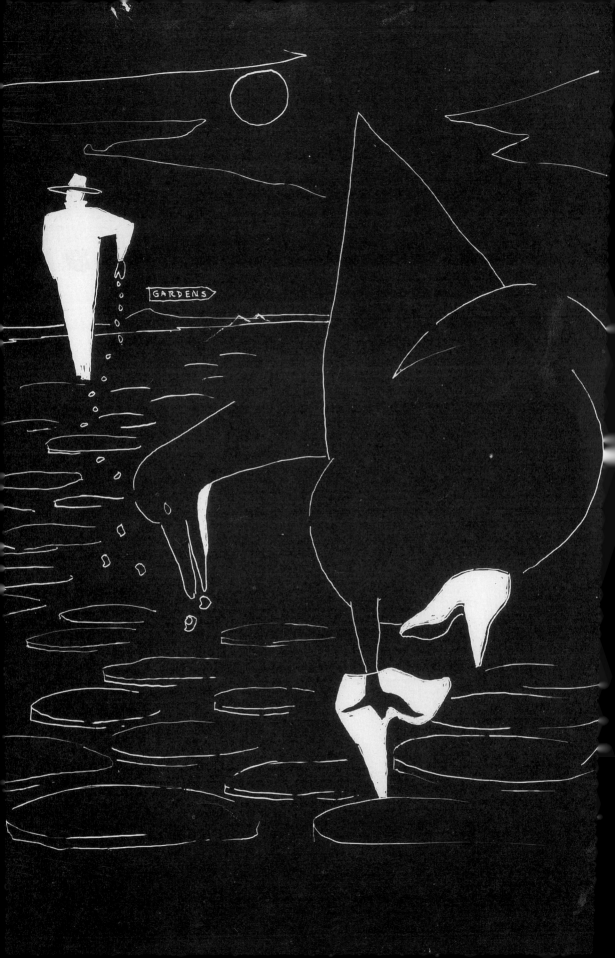

America, the Beautiful

I'm not going to tell you the way Americans walk. You know how that is. It's the *right* way, the natural way. But if I were going to be scientific about the American garden, I'd certainly start with the heels on women's shoes. I'd get a fellowship and do a paper called "An Analysis of the Influence of High Heels on Patterns and Industry in an Egalitarian Society." It would be a corker. No one would read it, but it would be a corker. Right now, we have no such study, and I have to admit that the question of what to do about women's heels and garden pavings is beyond me. Heels and paving. I've heard that song so much I'm used to its obscenity. But when I think about it I sometimes prefer the combination of "bombs and children." Certainly "barefoot and pregnant."

Just the floors of elevators are a gold mine of information. They've never found a material to cover the floors of elevators which could stand the push of women's heels. To begin with, let's say an American woman weighs about 120 pounds. That's what she says she weighs. Well, if she wears heels that measure a conservative half-inch across the base, she's in style, but the pressure her weight exerts on the floor is the equivalent of 240 pounds per square inch for each heel. That's when she's got the weight evenly distributed. If she happens to shift her weight all to one foot, the pressure is doubled, of course, or the equivalent of 480 pounds per square inch. Just to give you an idea of how much this is, I can tell you that the roof on an average house is figured to withstand a load of about 40 pounds per square *foot.* That's including the snow load. Well, at 280 pounds per square inch, the pressure exerted by just one of those heels under a 120-pound woman, standing still, with her weight evenly distributed, would be 34,560 pounds if it were figured the way you figure the probable load on the roof of your house—in pounds per square foot.

The heel pressure isn't applied over any large area like that, of course. It's applied to one-quarter of a square inch of surface, but the pressure is proportionate. When you add this to the pressure of the upward thrust of an elevator, you have an astronomical figure. This can easily double or triple, even quadruple, if the woman happens to shift her weight to one foot or weigh more than 120 pounds. The action is something like a bullet being shot into the floor, and the elevator companies have never found a material that could withstand it.

I find it pays to watch these little things if you're going to do gardens. It isn't just the pounds per square inch and all that, but there's a symbolism about them. They show what you're working with. For instance, I've never figured the pressure per garden stone when a woman is just walking in a garden. Not in pounds per stone. I don't think that's so important. It's those little spaces, between the stones. When she steps into one of those she makes a terrible noise, and that's where the pressure is. It's easily quadruple anything that could possibly happen in an elevator, and that little noise found in the great between is probably the most significant factor in shaping our environment. It's the "what" our gardens are.

This isn't as bad as it seems. It's just an American trait. Americans love to pose the impossible question. It tickles them. It reminds me of the old *Vanity Fair* cartoons, which used to show "impossible interviews" like Calvin Coolidge and Greta Garbo having a conversation. Americans loved it because it touched one of their basic traits. And it comes out in their gardens. It has to. It's part of the American character. They would like some dry rain so they could enjoy the sight without getting wet. They are capable of wanting, and sometimes getting, almost any impossibility. They come to you wide-eyed with the most absurd contradiction and a lump of "What do we do now" in their throats, and do you know this is the most hopeful thing I have noticed about them? They are in a dilemma and wide-eyed too. That's really hopeful. They're beginning to abandon those awful minds. They may eventually give up some of the other props, like Japanese stepping stones, or whatever their minds are anchored to at the moment.

One of the anchors is the "safety" complex. I began to think that nobody dies a natural death in America the way they're so afraid something will happen to them. They think that if they can just get things so that nothing happens to them they'll be perfectly safe and live forever, but that's an impossible situation that I don't think even an American can produce. There's a certain logic to it, though. The trouble is that the logic is outside of what *is*. Way out. The only way that I've discovered to fight that kind of logic is with logic. It's a counterirritant that sometimes works. For instance, one of the big impossible situations comes with the swimming pool. Everybody wants a swimming pool. I don't know why, but everybody wants a swimming pool. If anybody ever sat down with a pencil and paper and figured the cost per dip of having a swimming pool, he'd go on a screaming trip to the Sahara, instead. And save money. But nobody likes that kind of logic. It's no fun when you want a swimming pool. Logic is only fun when you have an impossible situation like how to have a swimming pool and avoid even the remotest possibility of anybody's drowning in it or falling into it when empty and cracking a skull. That's something to get your teeth into.

They've been working on that one for a long time. The pool companies, anxious parents, everybody. Anxious parents are the greatest. They have a special knack of keeping this logic game going forever. If their kids know how to swim better than they do, they'll borrow the neighbor's kids. If they have no neighbors for fifty miles, they'll invent a hypothetical kid. If that fails, there are always pets or wild animals or itinerant tramps. It's endless. I don't know what you do about it. I had mild success one time when I got so fed up with this logic game I was ready to offer myself as a sacrificial drowner. The game went on for days and days. I think the sentence that set me off was when the client said, "I'd just never forgive myself if a neighbor's kid drowned in our pool." They didn't even have the pool yet. They knew they were going to get one, of course, even if fifty kids drowned in it. They wanted a pool. That's how you play the game. So I said, very logically, "After all, there are so many kids and so few pools . . .," and that did it. They got their pool.

The interesting thing about this logic-torture is that it doesn't change anything. People get as many pools as they can afford, and safety has nothing to do with it. They just get very bad pools because they're so frightened, but pools they get. All those gates and locks and fences that make it a rich man's Coney Island are the sacrificial offering to fear. And this fear is another obstacle to ever getting anything like a Japanese garden or even a good garden. We try to make it safe, and that kills it. I'm not saying that gardens should be unsafe. That's the same thing. You can never make it safe or unsafe unless you are afraid of it.

The Japanese dote on water. They love it, and they're not afraid of it. It never occurs to them to put a fence around it because they're not afraid of it. That's an American idea, our way of seeing things. Actually, it's very hard to drown if your're *not* afraid of water. That's how it works.

But I don't want to spoil the fun. It hurts nice, if you know what I mean. It's a wonderful game. Tantalizing. And you don't always have to play it for life and death. You can even make the game safe. You can play for matchsticks. (Or toothpicks. They're safer.) I had a dilly of a client once who would play for anything safe. The lady was a perfectionist, of course. A real expert, though. Everything had to be done over three times. I don't know why it was always three. I suppose it had a symbolic meaning, but three seemed to satisfy her.

I didn't come in for much of it, but I used to feel sorry for the workmen. It's hard on a good craftsman when he meets an impossible situation and this particular job was full of them. The client used to drop in with the other ladies after lunch at the club, as was her wont, and hold court. She was looking for impossible situations. Little ones. The whole thing was an impossible situation, but she wanted little ones. The big situation was that the job was taking three times as long as it should because everything had to be done three times, and she'd complain about this and that put the workmen in an awful bind because they couldn't work while she was holding court because working made too much noise and they couldn't hear properly what she was saying about the way they weren't doing anything.

I just happened to pass by—almost pass by, anyway—at one of these sessions. I'm sure she didn't have anything impossible in mind for me—that is, nothing premeditated—but she was holding court and I was there and she wasn't the type to throw away opportunities like that. "What happens," she began—and I'm just *sure* that even after she'd got that far she didn't have anything in mind, just "what happens" and a long pause—but when you get that far, you've almost got a situation right in your hand. It's not impossible yet, but with the right person that always follows. I knew she had it when she started over—this time with an "Oh" and a pause before the "what happens" and a pause. Now she was launched. It was about a fountain-to-be, which she'd insisted should be in the center of a dining terrace table. It went like this: "Just suppose (pause) Mr. Perfection and I (pause) are all dressed for dinner (pause) and we've decided to dine on the terrace (long pause). We're sitting there (pause) and the fountain is going, mind you (medium pause), and then a breeze comes up (no pause) what happens?"

I'm afraid I did say it. It's the only possible answer to an impossible question. If you get yourself into that kind of a situation you're bound to get wet. But that isn't the point. The point is that you don't need a fountain or a terrace or anything else to play the impossible-situation game. In fact, they're almost mutually exclusive. Almost. It works that way if you don't really want a garden. If you do want a garden, and are just a victim of impossible-situation thinking in an impossible-situation culture, then the results can be very interesting if you find your way. Most people never do, but it is possible. In a way, it's the perfect situation. Painful but perfect. When you can't go either way, that's when you're likely to find the way. And it isn't the middle way of compromise and imitation and killing the goose and all that, either. It's the great "between." When that strikes, you know it.

Our Way

I don't know how water got so much into this. I think I started to say something about heels and paving, or perhaps it was about American gardens, but that's how it often happens. You start out with one thing and end up with another, but I've learned to trust this because so often in the end you find out you're talking about the same thing and, if you'd stuck to the original just because you'd started with it, you'd find out that that wasn't what you wanted to say. It would be very reasonable but miss the point entirely. So I guess I'll talk about water because water is important, and I don't know why.

I do know that no reaction is almost impossible about water. You can't be neutral about it. It's easy for a lot of people to be neutral about rocks, and they take the earth pretty much for granted. But water is different. Even people who don't like water are fascinated by it. They watch it like a natural enemy, but they watch it. Maybe it's because it's the hardest thing to capture, and presents a challenge. Oh, you can have water all right—as much as you can afford—but to get with it is a tricky business. You have to know how to see it. It's tricky. It's almost anything you want it to be and it's changing every second and all the while it's staying the same. That's why you have to catch it without capturing it, and that's a neat trick. You can't demand anything of it because it won't give you anything, but it's all there if you're with it.

I built a small lake once for some people who did and didn't like water. That was traumatic. They were afraid of "bugs"—that was the particular thing—but they were delighted that the lake had to be quite a distance from the house because of the way that the land fell. You could just get a glimpse of it from the house. What caused all the anxiety was that a lake is a fair-sized project, with dams and earth modeling, and this one turned into an upper and a lower lake with a dam between because of the way the land fell. This costs money and plenty of it and people get anxious about money no matter how much they have. So it was a much less painful day when the water came flowing in and decided to stay on the side of the dam we intended it to stay on. Everybody gathered for the occasion and not a single hand was being wrung, but it started to rain. Not much, but you can never tell about rain, so everyone dashed for the house, which was a long way for a dash. I had to stay at the lake to check a few points with the surveyor, and he said, "Look at that." From the way he said it, I realized he wasn't talking about surveying, he was talking about the water and the sky that was in it and the way the rain fell on it and the way the water circled out and how the people who had paid for it were scrambling back to the house and how it didn't even belong to them because they weren't with it.

I don't think the water cares. Water is like that. It never "courts" you. Some people don't like that about water, but that's the way it is. Very independent. And if you're going to be independent, too, you'll just never get with it, but everything is there if you do. If you see it one way—your way—it's a muddy hole where children drown and mosquitoes breed. If you see it another way, it's the universe. And whichever way you see it is the way you are. It *is* you, and nothing else. I don't care whether you're in Japan or Minnesota, that's what it is. And it isn't enough just to see that raindrops make concentric circles and water reflects the sky. Any idiot knows that. There's another step. You have to *be* the water and all the rest of it. Crazy? Sure it is. Now you're catching on.

I hope you don't think I'm trying to make water into some kind of a diety. I hope you don't even think that I'm talking about water. I'm not. I'm talking about you. The great American YOU who is always saying something like, "Water come to ME," and the water obeys. All you have to do is turn the faucet. It's magic. Well, that's your petri dish for you. No magic. No wonder you think you can pipe in Japanese gardens, too. Have you tried a Japanese moon? They're great. Gardens are kid stuff compared with a moon. That's *really* an impossible situation.

All the same, I can't help thinking that when things get that impossible, something's got to give. It's immovable and irresistible at the same time, and therefore fictitious—not at all the way it is down by the lake. Down there, you have to perform in your own petri dish. But you don't listen to it. You hear it without listening. You see it without looking—and now for the really crazy part—you're right on the edge and therefore can draw from both sides—nature and the petri dish. Then you do something that makes it neither nature nor petri dish while it's still both, except that it isn't either. You see? It's something new.

Now, don't ask me what the something is that you do because I don't know. You have to find that out for yourself and it may be different for you. It just happens, and I'm very happy about it so I don't look a gift horse in the mouth. It's the way that water is neither H_2 nor O, but a new thing which is both and neither at the same time. But it isn't as mechanical as that. I mean you can't set up a laboratory and put some nature in a big vat with petri jelly and get it. That's killing the goose again. You're dealing with variables that are never the same and always the same but it depends on when and where. That's why you can't take a little Japanese goo and some outside nature and get here and now. You violate where and when. Is that clear? I hope so because I want to get on to here and now which *is*. Do you see what I mean?

I don't admit it to everyone, but I get a little self-conscious talking about "that" and "what" and "it" all the time. I do it because I don't have to define them. But other words are different. They're embarrassing, sometimes. Particularly when you're talking to Mexicans or Canadians, it's embarrassing to call the United States "America," for instance. When you're talking with Americans—people from the United States —you always call it "America" unless you're Frank Lloyd Wright. Wright wanted everybody to call the United States "Usonia." In fact, he practically insisted upon it. And it's "very reasonable," as the Japanese would say, but it never caught on. It never attached itself to the main current of our culture. Wright always used it. He used it so much that his work became known as Usonian architecture, but that didn't get to mean either American or United States architecture the way he thought it would. It got to mean Usonian—a kind of local thing—like Hoosier. Ask any librarian what Usonia is and you'll find it's a place in America invented by Frank Lloyd Wright.

George Bernard Shaw had the same kind of peeve. He wanted everybody—or maybe it was only diplomats—to speak or write in Esperanto. I've often wondered what would have happened to Shaw's plays if he had written them in Esperanto. It would have been interesting—a sort of international style in playwriting like the international style in architecture. But Shaw didn't do that. He just told everybody else to do it the way that Wordsworth told everybody else how to write "poetry" and then ignored the whole thing himself and just wrote poetry.

There's something diabolical about the way that so many great men, consciously or unconsciously, try to get everybody else in a bind. Maybe it's just that they can't explain what they do and shouldn't try and yet they do try. I think it's a mistake, but it's a terrible temptation because everybody is always asking. Of course, it's a diabolical question and probably deserves a diabolical answer. But the answer is really in the question. That's how you do it. You just do it. I can't tell anyone how to do a garden. I'd have to say, "What garden? Where is it? Whose is it? Why is it? And when?" By that time, they'd *see* at least how I do a garden.

Right now, I find it difficult even to *describe* my own gardens. I'm not going to call them Usonian. That doesn't fit. Besides, everybody would almost certainly think I was trying to cash in on Frank Lloyd Wright, or at least that I was a follower of his—a trap which I suspect him of setting from the beginning—but at the very least we'd be back to "influences," and I just get tired around the eyes when I even think about it. I'm not going to call them American or United States gardens, either. *You* can do that if you want to, but for me to do it sounds too inclusive and pretentious. Besides, there are a lot of gardens in the United States that I don't want to be associated with.

So I've decided to call mine "gardens by an American." It isn't Esperanto, but everybody will know what I mean if they don't stop to think about it. That's important, not to think about it. That's where all the trouble begins. Look what happened to the centipede when some idiot asked him how he managed to walk with so many legs. He was doing very nicely until he stopped to think about it and then he couldn't walk at all. And if I think about calling my gardens "gardens by an American," I have to say well, not really "American" because of those Mexicans and Canadians to say nothing of Central and South Americans. "Gardens by a United Stateser," perhaps. Well, not really a "United Stateser," either. A Pennsylvanian, I guess, but a Pennsylvanian who has lived more outside of Pennsylvania than in Pennsylvania. Then I'd have to mention all the other places and "influences," and when I got all finished, you'd know less about what I meant than before I began because I don't mean geography at all.

I mean just who you know I mean. "Gardens by an American." Gardens by someone brought up in and conditioned by the very special and peculiar petri dish that got its mainline of jelly supply from England and Europe and has been myopically trying to find its way ever since. The "American" Indian and the Mayan and the Aztec cultures, which were closer geographically, had nothing to do with it. They were almost unmentionable in our petri dish. Neither did Japan or the rest of Asia have much to do with it. That's an intellectual idea that got into the books but never got into the family like a blood relative, except on Sunday afternoons when we like to display our finery. It's part of the word game which has practically replaced croquet.

I even saw a very serious book—that's the kind, the serious ones—that practically proved that Frank Lloyd Wright was really Japanese and not "Usonian" at all. Of course, it used the word "influence," and that's the trick. From there, you can go round and round on a wonderful chain that you've got so used to that you don't even think it's a chain anymore. It's a chain, all right, and one I'd like to avoid. You know perfectly well what I mean when I say "gardens by an American." I don't care what the dictionary says or what Frank Lloyd Wright says or even what the maps and the influential books say. You know what I mean. Everyone knows what I mean, particularly those who resent it, because what they resent is what I mean.

And it *doesn't* mean I'm going to tell anyone how to do an American garden. Boy, the magazines would love that. They'd give you "Gardens from Your Petri Dish" in four easy steps, and that would cook the garden goose so that it would stay cooked. The little oversight is that I'm not talking about "American gardens." I'm talking about gardens by one particular American. He's a guy I've come to know fairly well, and if you want to know how he goes about doing a garden, I think I can tell you. I can at least describe the motions. Maybe even give you some tricks.

I'm going to choose a specific example because I don't know anything about gardens in the abstract—that is, principles about garden making—and the example isn't even going to be a garden, exactly. Not because I'm mean. That's only part of it. But I don't want you thinking about your backyard while you should be concentrating on what I say. Not concentrating, either. Please don't concentrate. That's like thinking and it spoils everything. Just let yourself go with it for a while. You can always erase.

It's not so difficult to just go with it for a while, unless you went to Princeton. I say that because this is partly about Princeton. I tried the experiment with the Princeton boys—not all of them, just some of the upperclassmen in the architectural school—and it was a flop. They couldn't stop thinking. And when they tried to let go they *concentrated* on letting go. That's the way they are. They want to pick everything apart. They want to understand it—from the outside, of course—and that's how they can know what's going on without *being* what's going on, even for a little while, and that's why the experiment was a flop.

Maybe I was too anxious because I wanted the experiment to work. That's almost as bad as thinking about it. But with them thinking and me anxious to have it work, the experiment didn't have a chance. They're probably still thinking (about something new, of course), but at least I'm not so anxious about it anymore, and perhaps you'll see what I mean if you don't start thinking. Promise? Well, anyone who's ever been up in an airplane knows what one of those planned housing projects looks like. They've come a long way from cow paths. They're "architected" paths—tracks left in the landscape by all sorts of sophisticated instruments (tools, really) like T squares and triangles and drafting boards and telephone calls (God, the telephone calls), and bulldozers and trucks, and carry-alls and whatnot—all masterminded by some architect or planner or engineer or builder or city councilman or at least an "expert" or a combination of these in more or less democratic collaboration with anybody who wants to put in his two cents.

That's our way. There's a lot of thought that goes into it, even more dollars, to say nothing of principles and civic virtue and good intentions and talent—yes, talent—and all the rest of it. The amazing thing is the consistency of the forms that develop when you see them from just the right altitude to see them whole. They look just the way they did on the drafting board. They're *forms* made out of T-squares and triangles and telephone calls and bulldozers, laid down like the law of what we've convinced ourselves is *it.* Oh, the arguments! You can't beat them. They're logical and consistent and high-minded and and and. And, you can't beat them—if—if you accept their original premise that the purpose of it all is to make a cage for living—a cage for people to live in—not an ordinary cage, of course, but a very special cage where nobody knows who or what he is or whether the cage is supposed to keep him in or keep the enemy out and which side of it is he on anyway.

The thing I like about airplanes and flying is that sometimes you can get up high enough so that you don't see just the man-made part of it—the cage—as the whole. That's ground stuff, and it begins to blur after a while and you begin to realize that it isn't necessarily the whole story. Of course, you know perfectly well there are people down there, running around in those cages—and not just the architectural cages—doing all sorts of important things like yelling at children and writing books and making telephone calls so they can keep from knowing which side of the cage they're on. But soon the whole thing begins to look more like a rug, and you can see that even the largest vacuum cleaner you can possibly imagine isn't going to change a thing. They'd just find an anti-vacuum vacuum cleaner, and everything would be the same as before. But it isn't just that. It isn't just a rug that you can clean.

It isn't even a cage. That's all part of it, but the distance has nothing to do with it as long as you *see* it, and that it's only part of something else. You don't have to be five miles up in the air to see this. If you're going to see it at all, you'll see it from wherever you are. If you look at it one way, it's pretty remote from what you might call a garden—after all, a garden is made of stones and earth, plants and water (perhaps you will permit a little of the sky)—but if you look at it another way, it *is* a garden—the stones and earth and plants and sky are still there—but you can't tell that sort of thing to a Princeton man. He'll argue. He'll think about it. He'll compare it with other theories. In short, he'll *separate* himself from it, change it to a concept and mix it with a thousand other concepts he has stored away, toss them around in a mental shaker and serve as a refreshment at bull sessions. That's education, perhaps, but it isn't a garden. He doesn's *see* it. He simply knows what the words are saying.

Like all intellectuals—and some not-so-intellectuals—he has to be tricked. This is like delivering a good body blow to an expert boxer. I don't mean just to hit him when he isn't looking or when he has his guard down. That will do no good at all. He'll just spend more time at the gym to become more "expert." You've got to arrange for him to knock *himself* out. After that he *may* see something, but there's absolutely no guarantee. That's why I didn't ask the Princeton boys to "do a garden." You have to take off from what they know. Well, one thing they know is how to do a community. That's something you can really get your teeth into. Not just any old community, of course. That would be an insult to ask. These are near-architects, who've been "doing communities" for four or five years. They know how. It has to be something special with all sorts of thises and thats to whet the jaded appetite.

I don't know much about that kind of a community, so I let *them* work it out. (I would have, anyway—that's part of the trick—since they would probably feel I had imposed something on them if I had just given them a problem.) They worked out something quite interesting, I thought—something more or less in their own image—and I have to admit it wasn't bad. They're clever. It was "a village for working scientists"—not just ordinary scientists, of course—a little less than Einstein, perhaps—but still scientists who might be called to Princeton to carry on their work.

Now, when you get a bunch of scientists thrown at you to take care of, you have a problem. That's what we were looking for. And don't think the word "village" was arrived at rigidly or haphazardly, either. It was a tentative idea that a group of scientists working together—and separately—*might* become village-like (whatever that is), but one of the tricks, and a pretty important one, is to let it become what it wants to be. So we didn't pin it down—except for filing something in the Director's office. It was all terribly broad-minded.

You have to remember that any architectural school problem is in the nature of an experiment. It's impossible to duplicate the conditions outside. Some schools try to do this, but I think it's a mistake. You get the banker and the building inspector and the committee into the act, and they'll never act the way they really are in front of students, and students will never really act the way they would in front of a real live banker or committee, which they think might have the power to make or break their careers. It's different. How to handle a mock set-up becomes the problem. You could become very expert at handling mock set-ups—or real ones, for that matter—without having anything architectural to say. You'd be an entrepreneur, but not necessarily an architect. But there is a reality of sorts about a school problem. The reality is that it *is* a school problem. It has its own cage, and that's as good as any other cage if you want to find out who and where you are in it or outside of it or, if it isn't you, who or where is it. When you start borrowing mocked-up problems from other cages, you simply complicate the issue and are liable to get a mocked-up answer.

The academic experiment was good enough for the moment. At least we accepted it. It did have some advantages. It got rid of most of those objectionable people who always know a thousand ways that it can't be done. Now, you're looking at a blank piece of paper and yourself. Forget about the paper. You're looking at yourself. That's freedom, they say. But the scientists are coming. That's terrifying. You're an architect. Do something. Well, how many scientists? What kind? Where? I'll give you a hint. First of all, scientists are people. Don't laugh. They are, and you may have had a different idea. So let's talk about people, how they're taken care of (or should I say, taken in and done for?). I read a book once. I've forgotten what it said. It was all about "population density." I've even forgotten the figures. But I think the author was saying that if you could just regulate the number of people or families per acre you could get rid of slums. I don't think the jump was quite as broad as that, but it was something like that. So let's close the book and look out the window. I don't know whether you'd call what you see a slum or not. (I wish I could remember those figures.) Probably not. It's too respectable and expensive for that. Let's call it "suburbia U.S.A." That's just as good. It's a community of people. You'll find it's divided up in two or three different ways. It has a pattern. The pattern ranges from eight families per acre to one family per two acres. After that—in either direction—it gets to be something else, and we're not considering the "neediest cases."

Now, within each of these units—let's call them "units" whether they're eight to an acre or one to two acres—except for the size and the cost of the status symbols floating around, you find pretty much the same activity. It's a cycle. They have to eat, sleep, work, play. They have inside needs such as privacy, meditation, and intimacies, and outside needs, such as active recreation, social functions, and getting away from it all. There's also service and maintenance coming and going all the while. There are many more activities, both private and social, which I haven't mentioned. Please note that I purposely haven't mentioned kitchens, dining rooms, bedrooms, golf courses, or even gardens. These are already *forms* and therefore prejudicial. I haven't even mentioned "houses" for the same reason, although shelter is an obvious need. What I expect *you* to do is to take these scientists who are coming and provide for all their needs. There's just one catch. I want you to do it on a certain piece of property which is exactly the same size that would be required for eight families (really "houses") per acre except that—and here's the catch—I want you to *give* them something for it. That's all I have to say. That's all the professor you can make out of me. You're the architects.

We tossed it around for the next few meetings. It was a great group, full of curiosity, and I don't think I ought to mention which member of the faculty they had spinning on his ear trying to find out who was pulling all the pranks on the campus, but we used to talk a lot about that. I was quite surprised that we also got something like a program for the coming scientists. It just happened that way. We settled on a piece of property—a little less than twenty-four acres in the Princeton area—rectangular in shape (measuring 800 feet by 1200 feet). It was a theoretical piece of property with nothing particularly distinguished about it—the sort that builders use for developments. It was 150 yards from a turnpike leading to New York City and ten miles from the nearest urban center. The land had been lumbered recently and was bare with the exception of about an acre of dense woods along one of the borders. It had a stream which meandered diagonally across the tract which, of course, sloped gently in the same direction. You can see it anywhere in North Central Jersey if you get there before the builders.

Now bring on the scientists. To do that you have to "break it down"—that is, take it apart to see what you're dealing with. First of all, we decided to have a hundred of them. Not just because one hundred is a nice round figure, and makes a large enough group so that something can happen in a community sense, but also because one hundred (really ninety-six is exactly the number of houses that a builder would fit on that tract if he were figuring four houses to the acre on respectable lots measuring approximately 100 feet by 100 feet. There were,

95

however, slight differences. This was a working group with common interests. We assumed they were interested in their work and would rather have facilities which they could walk to on the site rather than commute. We, therefore, allotted nearly one acre to a research building or buildings. This, with the acre of dense woods, which was to be left undisturbed, reduced the amount of land to less than twenty-two acres instead of less than twenty-four.

We made other assumptions. First, that it was not the amount of land that surrounded one's castle, but the privacy it offered that was important. We also assumed (and this was cheating a little if you want to maintain an exact parallel with a builder's community) that twenty-five of these scientists would prefer, for one reason or another, to live off the site. We assumed that fifty of the scientists living on the site would have families (averaging 1.5 children per family, of course) and the other twenty-five members of the community would be single.

It worked out, if I remember correctly, that all the private land requirements for these scientists and their families—indoors and out—would be approximately six acres (twenty family units of 2500 square feet, thirty family units of 2000 square feet, and twenty-five singles units of 600 square feet plus an equal amount of outdoor space for gardens, terraces, etc.) This is considerably more than the effectively useable private space on a 100 feet by 100 feet lot in suburbia. This left sixteen acres for other uses.

One thing that developed as a great space-saver was community car parking and car storage. Even figuring two cars per family, this would amount to less than an acre in the total project. With parking grouped and accessible along the periphery instead of having internal roads and private drives as if the automobile were a diety, I can't even calculate the saving in space, maintenance, and the original expense of road-building, to say nothing of the accident hazards of mixing cars and children and the barren devotion to the mechanical god. This immediately left fifteen acres—much more than half the total space for a people-useful landscape.

This was a new situation. We spent many hours figuring out what to do with all that space that wasn't driveways or boundary to boundary front lawns. *That* was a real problem. Of course, you could always start a drugstore or a supermarket, but no one suggested it. (They knew they'd flunk if they did.) One of the suggestions was a central laundry in combination with a central heating system, which we incorporated immediately. I tried to stick to activities rather than forms, however, and the students came up with bicycling, supervised child play, gymnastics, horseback riding, skating, swimming, group gatherings, lectures, slides, recordings, demonstrations, and a host of other community rituals. We decided it would all be so attractive, that we would have to include guest accommodations for at least ten visiting dignitaries, restaurant facilities, and many other aids to hospitality. When they were all spread out, it looked like scrabble.

Now the trick. How are you going to organize all this, and at the same time, just let it happen? Well, have you ever just left the house and had the feeling that you were forgetting something? Good. Now, this time, leave that goddamn house—the one where all that junk about how things should be is stored and hope that you've forgotten *everything*. Then you've got the right attitude. Any idiot knows the sun comes up, and that's the most important thing that happens all day long and it didn't get an ounce of help from you, but if you're going to get with it, you'd better start thinking about that. Architects and planners have a fancy word for it. They call it "orientation." It isn't orientation at all, of course. It's the sun and how you are with it. It becomes the same thing as activity, what you do. And then there's another fancy word the architects use. Circulation. This means, can you do it? I mean without tripping over someone or something. Then you come to a lovely thing called "form." Everybody's all screwed up about this. You'll never get it. It's what's there and what isn't there at the same time. How's that for a conundrum? That's what "form" is. Then there's "use." Some call it "function," but it's really ritual—the ceremony of using something with respect. It's too much. Now all you have to do is bring all these things together—which should never have been separated in the first place— and you have what you're after. Some idiot is bound to call it "integration" or a "garden." You know how people are. They need words. As if the words were holding them together.

It's the words you have to get behind. They separate everything. Form, space, use, function, orientation. Even "integration." Boy, that's a laugh. Integration. It never has anything else until someone started poking around trying to find out what makes it tick. It just ticks and it doesn't need any help from you either. What are you trying to do? Hold the sun in the sky? Well, don't do it any favors. If you want to see how silly the words look when they're all lined up, here's what we've been talking about looks like in words.

I. Conditions of the site, considering its orientation
   A. External
      1. Connections to the outside—via turnpike to N.Y.C. and to local urban and shopping centers
      2. Resources—labor, mechanical equipment, money

3. Prospects—views, surrounding neighborhoods
    B.   Internal
        1. Water—meandering stream
        2. Slope—contour and elevation
        3. Inviolate—one acre of woodland, property boundaries
  II. Conditions of the problem (in terms of activity), considering each in relation to the sun
    A.   External—screen out or employ surrounding activity
    B.   Internal—house, private and community activity
 III. Circulation (resolving of conflict in movement), considering orientation
    A.   Dissection of movement patterns for study
    B.   Synthesis of same patterns in the environment
 IV. Form elements and space, considering sunlight and what it will do, ecology of it, man as part of the space, part of the environment
    A.   Earth—modeling, retaining, erosion control, paving
    B.   Water—containing or letting go
    C.   Planting and objects as part of the form
    D.   Structure as part of the space
  V. Ritual (use)—the test, how it can be used. Consider sun.
 VI. Integration. (That's the real trick. How you can bring all these people together without conflict, getting the most for each, permitting all the activity, relating these to the inside and the outside, considering the conditions of the site, of the problem, of movements, of things, of use—taking the astigmatism out of it as revealed by the layer by layer breakdown—considering the sun, how it moves.)

You see? You've got yourself another cage. A word cage. You should have seen how it trapped the Princeton boys. The Director had warned me that they were "great individualists," wouldn't collaborate on a problem and all that. So I let each one of them work out the problem individually. I gave them about two weeks to get it organized. I don't know what they were doing all that time. I thought it was already worked out. But they don't see things that way. They're intellectual, so that probably cogitated. I don't know. But they were very very busy, night work, and all that and I was quite happy about it because I could get rid of some non-cogitation of my own. But the day of unveiling had to come. I had to look at these drawings they'd cogitated about. They stood them up against the wall, and believe me it was just like being back on that airplane at the project height so that you could see it whole, but not whole enough. The Director hadn't told me they were all the *same* individualists out of the same mold as the individualist down there who kept making all those roady communities, the same ones over and over again.

They'd got the habit, and forgotten to forget everything when they left that awful house (you know the one). They kept thinking they were forgetting something and they weren't forgetting a thing. Everything was there, just as plain as it could be. Plainer. The driveways and the houses and all those "rational arguments" and the "economies" and boy, was it a mess. A real flop. I kept thinking how mortified most professors would be, and then I kept remembering that most professors might agree with them and that I wasn't a professor and that's how I saved myself. I looked as serious as I could, but I was really trying to gain time, and then I finally siad, "Let's just imagine this is an architectural office and I'm the bastard in charge, and you guys are working there and need the job so you'll do whatever I say." It was a polite way of telling them they weren't any longer individualists, but they agreed to the experiment.

I guess, in a way, I rough-housed them into doing it my way. That's pretty hard for individualists to take, but they were good sports about it. I certainly couldn't take seeing the same thing I see in airplanes all over again. I'm not the right kind of an individualist for that, I guess, so I started saying do this and do that. The first thing I did was take away those damned T-squares and triangles. I even took away pencils and paper. (This was all symbolic, of course, like washing your mind before the tea ceremony. I have nothing against T-squares or triangles except when you start thinking with them. After that, you've *got* to wash your mind). I was anxious, I guess, about all those scientists coming and the time slipping away, and that's always a poor start.

Anyway, I got the boys to build a big box—it must have been eight feet wide and twelve feet long—large enough to fit the whole property if one inch were equal to ten feet. That's the way you've got to do it if you want to see all the parts at once and make sure you don't have any left over at the end. Some of the boys even figured out how far up on a ladder you would have to climb to see it actual size as you would from an airplane. I'm not that good at mathematics, but they were and they enjoyed it so I let them do that in exchange for filling the box with sand. We needed the sand so we could push it around the way you would push the earth around with a bulldozer on the actual site. A T-square is the wrong thing to use for this. Hands are good.

The first encounter (on a very gentlemanly level) with the students was about what to do with all the land the analysis showed we had left over. There were a lot of suggestions. I can't remember any of them. I probably wasn't listening. That gets to be a habit. Finally, I said, "Let's build a lake." I had in mind that meandering stream that was running diagonally through the property and seemed to be going to waste. Anyway, I like lakes. Some of the students had used "water" in their own schemes, but I meant a *lake*. When I showed them the size I had in mind, they thought I was joking. Well, I was and I wasn't. We had nearly fifteen acres left over, and I didn't see any reason why at least half of it shouldn't be used for a lake. That would be big enough for sailboating and swimming and ice-skating in the winter and it would be a wonderful place to float a raft with musicians playing on it in the summer evenings. It could border a promenade or a community restaurant or dining terrace and turn into a canal or start with a waterfall or just prevent someone from putting up that drugstore. Anybody knows what it is about a lake. At the very least it gives breezes and reflects things and that alone is enough reason to have a lake. (I hope that if developers should happen to read this, which isn't likely, they don't get the idea that the answer to the community problem is to have a lake. It isn't, and it doesn't pay, either, so perish the thought.)

Anyway, I was boss now, and I could see the scientists having a great time with the lake and all their wives worried to death about the children drowning, so we had a lake. As it turned out, we had two lakes—an upper and a lower—because of the way the land fell. They were connected (or separated) by a causeway, which was the dam between and provided a promenade as well as a waterfall, and the lower lake could be set at different levels by means of a lock arrangement. This meant that the water level could be adjusted to reveal a couple of islands— disappearing islands, I guess—when you wanted to have it that way, and the upper lake was more for fishing or sailing. You have to give people this sort of nonsense so that they'll have something to "think" about and so that they'll think it's practical, and leave you alone. For my own part, I'm perfectly content with a lake that's just a lake on all sides and lets the moon reflect in it without worrying about what kind of lake it's going to be.

Of course, there all kinds of lakes. The terrible ones are usually the ones where people have worried them into being something else entirely—a mixing bowl for motor boats or a cook-out spot for city campers—but I just had an idea this would be a good lake, or rather, two lakes (and that none of the scientists would ever, ever all it "Twin Lakes"). It would just be a couple of lakes doing what lakes ought to do, things like keeping drugstores out and having some people on the other side and letting—that's the most important part, the letting—the moon come in.

Well, we finally got the project completed. Not exactly on time (that's the way it is when you're working for a boss), but I will say the

students did a beautiful job of model-making. It had housing for as many people as you could reasonably get on the same property in Suburbia, but they had something—they had privacy, they had a community where things could happen—all the human activity to be with it. I'm not going to recite all the things you could do in such a community because to do do do is not the point. The real test, I suppose is whether you could do "nothing," and I think you could. It fitted. It had many faces, and depth for each—children, work, play. The night, the moon, the sun. The face of ceremony, ritual, and being alone. You could go as far as you were capable without interference from the environment. That's quite an achievement. I call it a garden.

I don't think I have to read you the third act from Hamlet to show you that it was no more like the T-square–triangle–"architected"–builder's–development teepee that so many Americans live in than I to Hercules—although, on second thought, that might have been just the thing to do for the Princeton boys. Apparently they didn't see it. Perhaps they had really knocked themselves out, after all. They were a good lot. Nice boys, all of them. I couldn't understand it. There they were all standing around looking at the model. I was standing there too. Some of them were up on a ladder and others were on the scaffolding peering down at the model at the proper distance just as though they were up in a plane, but not moving. They were seeing it whole, but not whole enough, I guess, because nothing was happening. I'd never seen that before. It's a terrible thing to see—a bunch of young men all standing around and nothing happening. I began to get sick of that model. As nice as it was, it made me sick because nothing was happening.

I was ready to throw in the sponge and mop up the remains of a bad job. I couldn't bear to look at that model any more so I started looking at the boys. They were a good lot all right, but I realized I hadn't seen them before. They'd knocked themselves out, and they hadn't come to standing yet. They weren't standing at all. Oh, they were "standing" alright, everywhere and on everything and they were "looking," but the inside of them wasn't standing. You may not think that has much to do with a garden, but that *is* the garden. You've got to know how to stand. No one in the world can tell you how to do it. You've just got to *know* how to stand. It's got to happen to you.

Of course, any idiot knows how to stand, but I'm not talking about that. It's not that it's difficult, it's that it's too simple and there are too many things in that cage that keep you from seeing how simple it is. You need a lake somewhere, but it's even simpler than that. You don't even need a lake. You just need to stand there beside it. It would be nice to have a moon there, too, but you don't need the moon because it's always there. What you need is to *know* it's there, and I don't mean to think about it or to measure the distance or to make a rocket. I mean you've got to *come to standing*. It's not something you do, it's something you are. It has nothing to do with whether you went to Princeton or not. It's something between you and the moon and the lake. And when you've come to standing, you *know* it because there isn't any moon and there isn't any lake, but most of all there isn't any YOU. You're all the same. You're with it. It's too simple. It's a miracle. You know the glory of it because there isn't any difference. There isn't any cage. That's the inside and the outside of it. It's the way a peony does. It's the way the lake does and it's the way the moon does. That's where the garden is— when you've come to standing—here and now.

103

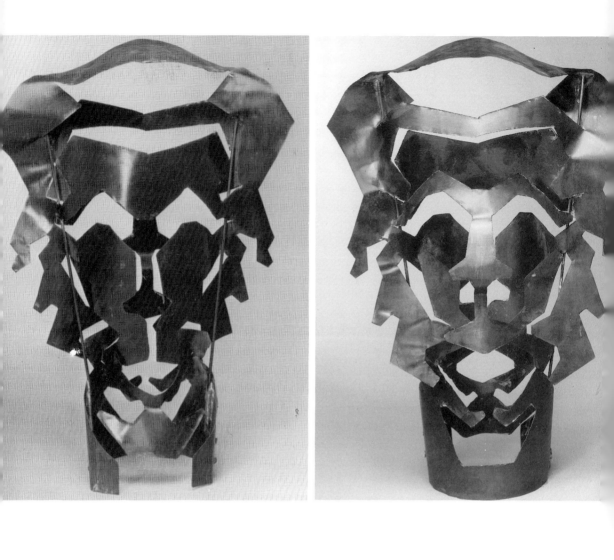

East in the Morning, West in the Afternoon

And all this while YOU thought a garden was for flowers, a place of lavender and old lace. How far out can you get? Who knows anything about flowers in this petri dish or who has any time for them? And where are the flowers in the Ryoanji, which everybody keeps saying is the greatest garden? Where are the flowers at the Villa D'Este, come to think of it, and why isn't a garden just a collection of words, anyway? Or is it? Perhaps it isn't there at all, perhaps it's everything the way it is.

It seems to me that I've been distressingly clear up to now, I really owe you a little confusion. Not ordinary confusion, of course like the confusion between East and West, but that special day-to-day stuff. It has nothing to do with Asia or the western world. I'm talking about the points on the compass—really about how I once tried to put my finger in the dike of every landscape problem in suburbia. Well, not *all* suburbia. But most of Long Island, Westchester County, Connecticut, and points north, south, east, and west. What a mistake! I used to rush from morning until night from one job to another, like a country doctor, and all I remember of it now is that no matter how I tried to plan my days, I was always driving into the glare of the sun—east in the morning, west in the afternoon.

Sometimes I'd "do" as many as four or five landscapes a day, never fewer than two. You see, I really mean it when I say it's easy or quick or no problem. All you have to be is crazy enough to do it. And if you're crazy enough to go spinning around with the sun continually in your eyes, you're crazy enough. You have the sensation of working in a Bull-dog Drummond series. You can't tell which picture you're in. There's something like that about suburbia, and the something is the sameness. Of course, I know that *yours* is different (and it's all the same to me), but you still have that house and that driveway and that builder and those kids and that lawn and those neighbors and all your precious ideas, preventing anything from happening.

I've cheated a lot of people into letting something happen, but boy, it's just a finger in the dike. It doesn't pay. I know. I'm always hearing about jobs I've done somewhere, and I can't even remember them or the name of the people. Sometimes the reports are good, and sometimes they're terrible, but I always get full credit. I probably dashed out to somebody's house because of one of those telephone calls, and maybe spent a couple of hours trying to straighten out the mess, and a couple of years later I'd discover that it was *mine!* It's like the day that Sousa walked down the street and heard an organ grinder playing his "Stars and Stripes Forever." It dragged so pitifully he couldn't stand it, so he introduced himself to the organ grinder and showed him how to play it at the proper tempo. The next day the organ grinder had a sign on his chest that read "Pupil of John Philip Sousa."

I don't care about that. That isn't the real mistake. The real mistake is in going back. You should never go back. I know that as well as anyone. I got tricked into it one day when I was out with a photographer and he thought it would be fun to see what had happened to all these places after eight or ten years. That's how it happened. I think the weather was partly to blame. It was that in-between time of spring when nothing has made up its mind, a gray day.

The way you know you're coming to a place is that you see imitations on each side. You can't convince people that just because they get the same goods they won't necessarily have the same dress. They pick up, or pick "out" something that's part of something else and put it on their lawn expecting to have the same thing. It's amazing. In this particular community, which was on Long Island, I must have done 30 or 40 places and there must have been a 140 imitations. I say I "did" the places. I really consulted with the owners and pointed them in a direction—sometimes quite specifically with diagrams and sketches and some-times not so specifically—and then they'd carry on by themselves with varying degrees of success. Sometimes they'd call me back to help them each step of the way, and sometimes they'd get bogged down with the nursery or a contractor, and I'd never hear from them again.

This isn't exactly the same thing as taking a job through from the beginning to the end. I'm not a perfectionist about that. Some people are. They like to put a bell jar over their work, as if it were going to be exhibited at a museum, but I don't have any feeling about it one way or the other. I can't think of it as a "creation" that one tries to preserve. It's a process that starts wherever you are and never ends. Of course, it's very nice to get there before the dam breaks. It's even nicer if you can get there before the builder or the banker or the inspector loads the dice against you, but you have to get up pretty early for that. You're dealing with something that's already in motion and is likely to remain in motion after you've left and you've got to go with it, because no matter where you start, it isn't the beginning and no matter where you leave off, it isn't the end.

There's a rhythm, and I don't object to that—not the natural one. It goes and goes and goes, and then it comes back again. There's nothing to lose and nothing to gain. It's trying to put it under a bell jar or capture it or put it in a cage or outside a cage so that you're on the other side, whichever that is, instead of letting it come and go and being with it. I've heard it said that you can't tie a garden to a "philosophic statement" like that—it's too broad a jump—and, of course, you can't, and it is too broad a jump if you've already so separated everything that a philosophic statement is an arrangement of words in a book and what *happens* is a different matter entirely. A garden *is* a philosophic statement. You don't have to "tie" it to words. It shows which side of the cage you're on and which side nature's on—and so does that "house" and that development (I mean community) and all the other junk in the cow path and don't try to be so "innocent" about it, either. You know perfectly well innocence doesn't work. Not in this petri dish.

The rhythm is one thing, and the devices people will use to stay outside it is quite another. And if you don't want to see this impossible situation in action, don't look right or left. At least don't look at any community I know of in this country. The only thing you'll see holding it together is the road system for automobiles. The houses are making faces at the streets. They're masks. And with that greenery pretending to be an English lawn in front, you'd never guess that anything happens behind it. Nothing like people living, I mean. Oh, you see them around, getting in and out of cars and buying things at the supermarket, but where do they live? Where do they get with it?

They want to get with it, of course. But most of them don't have the faintest idea how. It's an atrophy. An atrophy and a cage. They think a garden is another cage like the "house" and, of course, it is. Or it can be. It depends which side you're on. Little things are terribly confusing.

Just how far do you go with this nature bit? Well, I don't know. Just how frightened are you? A neighbor, kibitzing a job where I was saving a wild cherry tree—for one thousand and one reasons like it was the only tree, it fell in a good place, had a beautiful shape, gave shade, and the owners couldn't afford to replace it—said, "Well, if that were mine, it's the first thing I'd get rid of." I didn't doubt her word, but I couldn't understand what she had against the cherry tree. When I asked her, she said, "Bugs?" as though I should have known all along. And it wasn't so much what she said as the startled terror in her face, as if she were already crawling with vermin at the thought of it, and it wasn't even *her* tree and it didn't have any more "bugs" than any other tree as far as I could tell.

I'm sure this lady's own back yard was much more antiseptic than the one I left the neighbor with. That was one of the few small gratifications in going back after a few years. Hers was still antiseptic, and in her neighbor's something was happening and I don't mean "bugs." By some

small miracle the bugs never did come. Perhaps the birds kept them
away. There were a lot of birds, but the antiseptic lady wouldn't have
liked them either, I suppose. Another small gratificaton was that the
whole community—imitations, the antiseptic lady, and all—had begun
to take on a crazy kind of unity. It wasn't much, and pretty spotty for the
most part and it wasn't of the highest order, but here and there you
could get a glimpse of something happening. You could sense there was
some kind of living going on, and it wasn't making faces at the street.

I don't know why this was so. It just happened, I like to think. I'd like
to make a guess, but that's dangerous. Someone would be sure to latch
on to it and reduce it to "Six Rules for Making a Development into a
Community," and I don't think there are any "rules"—at least not that
kind. You'd have to get a new developer, get rid of that foundation plant-

ing and save that cherry tree. That would be a beginning—not the real beginning, but a start. Then you'd have to try for privacy—not isolation—just privacy, and yet make the connection. The next thing you'd have to do is look into that nearly perfect mirror at the exact moment you say, "bugs" and try to see what it is that isn't there that frightens you. In time (a long time) you might get used to the obscenity of a compost heap. I can just see YOU in that uniform and station wagon, collecting fallen leaves in autumn (uniform to match) for the "leaf bank" as part of the community drive. You're so earthy, my.

Of course, it would be nice to find a scapegoat. If you really need one, I propose the developer. That's silly, of course, because he only does what you tell him to do. He's just like the banker and the building inspector. (You're not so innocent yourself—not nearly innocent enough.) If you want a specific developer to start on, there's one up around New Rochelle. I don't know his name, and I probably never would have thought of him again except that that same photographer (perhaps he's the real culprit) inveigled me into going up there to look at another community where I'd done a lot of landscapes in the same way. I didn't want to go. All I could remember was how beautiful it was before the developer came in and blasted the natural rock—mountains of it—so that he could string suburbia on a skewer like shishkebab. The only satisfaction I could feel was that he probably lost his shirt in doing it. But he did it, of course. That's the only way he knows. And there I was again, making like a Dutch boy, with my finger in the dike.

It's completely out of character for me. I'm not that type. You have to have windmills and blond hair cut with a bowl. I'd like to do something but it would have to be more drastic—more like the Japanese boy who burned the rice fields because he saw the hurricane coming, and when all the people ran up the hill to right the fire, they were saved from the hurricane. It's a pleasant thought. But you can't go around burning suburbia. You can plunder it and blast it, sterilize it, and shoot the Indians —or whatever they're shooting in suburbia these days—but you musn't burn it. That's illegal. Even if a hurricane is coming. *After* the hurricane, you may put your finger in the dike—that prevents floods— if you do it in the approved manner. The approved manner is to find someone who can afford to decorate the path of the hurricane (formerly, the cow path), and that's where the luxury of it all comes in.

Anyone will tell you landscape architects are only for the rich. Of course they are. Hurricane fighting is expensive. Preventative landscaping is cheaper, but not nearly so exciting. Besides, it's out of character. We like things separate—something for when you can "afford" it—never part of the process. Nature becomes like that "natural" bridge—I think it's in Virginia—that you have to pay to see. It's fenced off—something you take school children to look at on Friday afternoons—a curiosity, not at all like school children. By the time they're old enough to build that dream house in Westchester, they may even have "gone to see" a tree (if they can afford it).

That reminds me. I didn't finish telling you what happened with that client who was so wonderful "except"—the one who didn't like apple trees any more when he discovered they had apples and that anything that would have apples would probably have yellow jackets. Well, he went right ahead and built nearly the whole garden, except for the place where the apple tree was to have been, and after a while it got to look as though it just *had* to have an apple tree. Even the client could see that, but he couldn't remember what the apple tree looked like so we had to go back to the nursery and look at it again. I didn't think it would still be there, but it was—they hadn't sold it—but it could have been an entirely different tree because the client didn't remember what it looked like at all. It was broad and flat and twisted and so low we would have to put it in a box so that you could walk under it, but the client didn't remember any of that—only that it had yellow jackets, which it didn't.

But by now, the garden had become a different thing, more in the client's image. At first, I'd thought of it as having a kind of bucolic quality. That's what the place seemed like to me. An apple tree is like that, somehow, with kids playing around it—a place where a farmer might feel at home. But this wasn't the client's image of himself, although he was relaxed-looking and stressed the kind of democratic simplicity sometimes found in people who act so much like the common, ordinary run of men that you know they're anything but common and ordinary. This should have been my cue, of course, but I didn't get it until after the apple tree bit. I sometimes take people for what they say they are, but I learn. You have to aim at something in a general way before you can bring it into focus.

Perfection was the real focus here. I know the symptoms. I knew he wasn't going to want the apple tree even after he saw it for the second time (which was really the first time for him). Even if the yellow jackets and the dropping apples had never come into it, I could tell by the way he wanted every nut and bolt in place and the way his wife kept asking whether brick would be "dusty." He didn't want an apple tree. The problem was that by this time the rest of the garden was mostly completed and the apple tree had begun to look better because it was cheaper than "perfection," and this always brings on a quandary.

In wandering around the nursery we saw several other trees which would do for his situation. Eventually, the choice narrowed down to just three—the apple tree was one, of course. We also saw an enormous winged euonymus—sometimes called the "burning bush" because in the fall of the year the colors seem to flame–which is really a bush, but this one was as large in outline as the apple tree, and I could see how it could be pruned and shaped so that it would be spectacular in that box instead of the apple tree. You've got to be able to see those things. You've got to be able to see how a scrubby little plant hidden and crowded in the woods or in a field, looking like any other, would be if someone cared enough to let it become what it wanted to be.

The third choice—which was certainly not third in order of beauty—was a dwarf Japanese maple, which I'm not even going to try to describe. It's the sort of thing you have to get with and I wish everything were as easy to get with as that. You don't need to bring anything with you and you don't need to read a book. It's just there, and boy, you know it. If you've never been wondered by anything, you owe it to yourself to sit under a dwarf Japanese maple and let its branches twist the sky for you and just go with it for a while. You'll never be the same again, and I mean that's a break.

Anyway, we had these three trees—the apple, the euonymus, and the maple—and now came the choice. That's the quandary. By some miracle, the apple was still there, ready to be loaded on the truck. The euonymus was (or could be) spectacular. Off-beat. No one else would have anything like it (it also had the advantage of costing about half as much as the apple). And there was the maple, smiling like a Buddha, asking nothing, but costing (as things go in this cruel world) twice as much as the apple. Now, I'm not going to tell you which one the client took. Not just because that isn't the point, but because I don't know. (That's how hot all this is.) The client is still deciding. He's "thinking" about it—the pros and cons, you know. I have a good idea which one it will be because I could feel something happen to him when he saw the maple. But then, he *saw* the apple tree this time. He also "understood" about the euonymus. So I'm not sure which one he will take. There are a lot of other considerations. I just handed him a mirror. What he doesn't know is that he isn't selecting a tree at all. He's selecting himself. That's a quandary and I don't know how it will turn out. All I know is that my own secret tree (the one I told you about) was just a stone's throw away, but I didn't show it to him. He might have bought it.

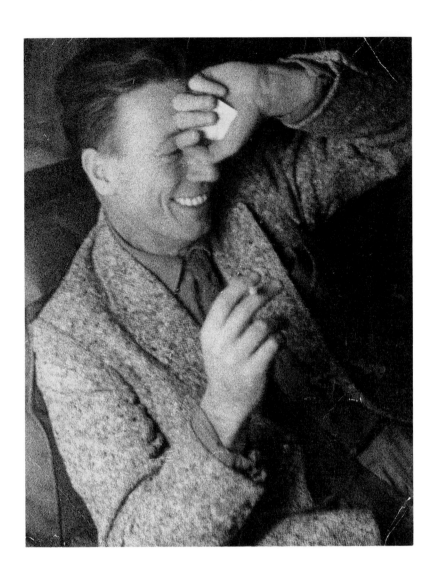

Epilogue

I'm almost afraid to say anything more definite about gardens. YOU latch on to everything so. I'm afraid you'll go around telling the neighbors that the whole secret is in finding the right tree (and boy, if you can just find *my* secret tree, you've got the secret of secrets). That's the way you are. I keep telling you there *is* no secret, and you think I'm kidding. I'm not. Well, just a little bit. It's only a secret when you've got yourself so walled off from it that it seems to be "outside." There may be hope. I don't know. The landscape wasn't so bad before you started "thinking" about it. I mean those barns and corncribs and silos, down through Pennsylvania, which just happened because no one was trying to make them something like "American Gothic," or to show who they were. Sometimes when I see a corncrib I could wish I were an ear of corn, they have it so good. Of course, you don't have to go that far. There's a people hope. It's something like treating people with the respect a farmer does an ear of corn. You think that's bad? Just look at that lake you worried into a mixing bowl. Look at Suburbia.

Let's try an experiment. Let's take a piece of property in Suburbia (I have a particular one in mind, but you choose your own. They're not so different.) Let's say it has that house on it already and the developer has long since departed. The lot, of course, is one hundred feet by one hundred feet. A typical lot. Of course, it's not an ordinary, typical lot, because the natural contour of the land rises steeply up hill toward the rear. Now instead of imposing a "garden" on this site, let's say we simply sculpture the land—make a carving, as you would if you were doing a bas relief of something you cared about (an ear of corn if you're a farmer)—to show its form more clearly. Not so much! Don't change it all around so I can't recognize it. Just make it more of what it already is. Don't you see that place that's almost level? Well, make it level, so you can use it. What for? . . Oh, you mean what do you use it for. Well, you tell me. You started this. Just be as specific as you can (you're good at that), but make it fit. . . . Not that way, stupid . . . make it fit the land and the use . . . watch that tree! That's another level. Boy, I wish I'd never started this. . . . Of course I know it's your property (you won't find me in Suburbia). You can do whatever you damned well please. Plant a lawn, if you want to. See if I care. . . . But don't talk to me about pavings until you take those heels off, and know what the ground is. . . . Planting . . . ? Of course. . . . That's what makes the levels into spaces. . . . I know. . . . You didn't get that . . . spaces are grown up forms (see page 97—the "silly" page). . . . They have sides, you're *in* them. . . . No, that isn't Japanese. They wear slippers. . . . You see? You're *in* something. . . . No, no "pictures!" . . . Get a painting, if you want pictures. . . . This, you look through. It's the interspatial vista (try that on the garden club). . . . Now do you see? Walk around. . . . See how it changes? I mean, *it* changes as *you* move. . . . You, too? Never! . . . Really? I don't believe it. . . . Not YOU. Gee, that's a gift. . . . the fourth dimension, I guess. . . . Imagine YOU, floating around in the fourth dimension, and not a flower in sight. . . . What's that? . . . Of course I know it's still Suburbia! Boy, sometimes. . . . *I* didn't make Suburbia. YOU did. At least now you're with it. . . . Maybe you'll get with. . . . Oh, no. . . . not YOU. . . .

Well, I'm glad that's over. It reminds me of something I'd rather forget. You know—east in the morning, west in the afternoon. Boy! When I was a kid in Pennsylvania, back on the farm—not the suburbs—they used to have something like that for chickens. It was pretty simple. It was a kind of cage. Not an ordinary cage, of course, but one with an electric light bulb in it. Well, chickens aren't very smart. If you put an electric light in their cage when the sun goes down, they can't tell whether it's day or night. They think it's morning already. And even though they've laid one egg in the real morning, they'll lay another in the electric-light-bulb morning. Well, the suburban cage is like that if you always go dashing around with the sun in your eyes. You drop a lot of gardens.

I don't know whether the chickens ever cracked wise or not, but I did—after a while. Of course, just because you crack wise, it doesn't mean you know what to do about it. I didn't. But something always happens (if you let it). And just about that time I got an invitation from the Japanese government to come to Japan for a visit. (Boy, did that invitation look pretty.) I hate to keep coming back to the Japanese all the time. (You notice that I don't keep coming back to something called "Japanese gardens".) They don't have any secret. They don't even have any non-secret. Yes, I know. You think they're kind of dumb. Well, not really dumb, but dumb enough to become like YOU when they finally "see the light!" It'll be difficult. They'll have to think about it, and I'm just betting that never "takes." They're not *that* dumb.

I knew that from the first Japanese I ever met—in Shemya of all places. Just being in the Aleutians is something of a shock. I don't know exactly how I got there—just one of those terrible mix-ups you get into traveling around, I guess. If it happens to you in the Aleutians, you never have to ask anyone what a rock is. It's the Aleutians. If you're unlucky enough to get on the wrong plane for Japan (probably there's still some of that morning or afternoon sun in your eyes), that's where you find yourself. Refueling, and all that. It only takes an hour or so in measured time, but you get a good glimpse into what eternity can be like.

I wouldn't be a bit surprised if the Japanese arranged all this. They're so good at getting you in the mood for what's to come. They want you to see the Aleutians first. Then you're ready for anything. There's a Quonset hut there. It's all fixed up. It's a regular day club. They've got coffee urns and tablecoths and pine-needle souvenirs and maple furniture bathed in amber light where you can just sit or write a postcard back home telling the folks what a great time you wish you were having. The personnel look like yesterday's liberty, and outside, the landscape goes on and on like suburbia's tomorrow. It's a wonderful prelude to Japan.

I was wandering around among the coffee pots and souvenirs, not thinking of anything in particular. I remember I had a postcard in my hand, but I couldn't think of anything to say or anyone to say it to. Everyone else was wandering around. There wasn't much else to do. And there wasn't much space to do it in because of all that maple furniture and the souvenirs and the coffee pots, and that's how I met my first Japanese. It was a strange experience. I forget whether it was between a coffee urn and a pine-needle cushion or between an amber light and an inner look, but things were crowded—no room to pass—and this Japanese couple was standing there. Not just standing their, either. There was a readiness and an agony about the way they stood—like a deer at the edge of the woods—then in a subliminal flash, too brief to count, when I was aware of being sized up. I think I passed inspection. They didn't say anything, but I could tell by their eyes. They weren't eyes at all. They were fringes of the Vermont woods the way Robert Frost saw them—wild and civilized—of the wilderness and of the person. No separation. I had to laugh. I'd always had the western notion (naturally), that it was just a matter of time before the Japanese would see the light—our light—and it wasn't that way at all. What was there went back and back and back, almost to the beginning. You didn't have to "think" about it. It was there. I had to laugh. It was ludicrous to think of them seeing our "light." It would be like bluebirds appearing at the polls some Tuesday morning in November to cast a vote.

Perhaps that day will come. I don't know. We're doing such wonderful things. I can't wait to see. I mean it. I can't wait—I have a date with a rock, and you know how *they* are. So, 'bye now. Don't think it hasn't been wonderful. It's been quite an experience. Wild, if you know what I mean. Wilder, if you don't . . . I can't explain it. But that's the best part of the joke, don't you think? You can never explain it. You've got to see it. No one can tell you. . . . It's like a play. . . . I thought you were simply hilarious as YOU. . . . But there are a lot of things I still don't get. Are YOU the moon and I the water? Ot is it the other way around? And where are YOU when I turn my back? In the mirror, still? Who do you fence with *then*? I don't understand. . . . Have I invented YOU, or did you think *me* up? Could we exist alone and separately? Or are we one and the same after all?

Anyway, I hope to find the exit while I'm still laughing. It's been such a wonderful joke. . . . Kept me in stitches almost *too* long. So many laughs. . . . A JOKE, really. Cosmic, you know, and all that. That's the best kind. . . . No, no. . . . I *loved* your petri dish. . . . Really I did. . . . Aw, c'mon now. . . . You're not going to be YOU again, are you? I think you have a wonderful petri dish. . . . no doubt a lifetime's supply of goo. You must come and see mine sometimes. . . . It's not really a petri dish, at all. . . . It's NOTHING, really. . . . Oh, not just an ordinary *nothing*, of course. . . . It's a very special. . . .